DAD JOKES

WORD SEARCH

PORTABLE
PRESS

San Diego, California

Portable Press
An imprint of Printers Row Publishing Group
9717 Pacific Heights Blvd, San Diego, CA 92121
www.portablepress.com • mail@portablepress.com

Publisher: Peter Norton • Associate Publisher: Ana Parker
Art Director: Charles McStravick
Senior Developmental Editor: April Graham Farr
Editor: Angela Garcia
Production Team: Julie Greene, Rusty von Dyl

Cover Design: Rosemary Rae
Interior Design: Traci Douglas

ISBN: 978-1-64517-733-3

Printed in the United States of America

25 24 23 22 21   1 2 3 4 5

PRACTICAL JOKES

```
D O O F C Z J Y Z B P K W K E G W N Q Z
L D C F A X W J E Z D E T V P Y N U X R
Q F B X Z D X B W I K A R M B T J W W N
T L D N O Z Q N K S O P X P E G G A M R
U N M F O O L I S H R R F E L P R A N K
M Z B L H J S S X J I I K A H E B C G U
Z B S A H Q Y N O C H L F T L B X F K S
T C B Q L M P W X D H F S Q Y Q N W J B
J S W G B R L O K L Y O T P D Y Z D W E
F R G L G B S L V Z Y O R Y D A M U S E
A S B M M T O C H N C L B A H M P K M M
A X U Q C F J E Y L H S R Y N C U T S A
Y N D E P M I S C H I E V O U S V T X F
O L J W X Q T D D E S S A R R A B M E W
M B G O A R N Q F W K D O U K Z P C Z J
O I U A G U M K G B B C N K M I S A I P
L L A C E N O H P Z V D F A H U W E Q L
L J E U G P L V H F E Z S A Q G Z D F O
E K A A A O V T V B K W O U L H P O G T
R V S A N T I C P V X C A J H J U T Q J
```

AMUSE	EMBARRASSED	MISCHIEVOUS
ANTIC	FOOD	OBJECTS
APRIL FOOLS	FOOLISH	PERPLEX
CLOWNS	GAGS	PHONE CALL
DARE	GAS	PRANK

Q: Did you hear about the crazy pancake?
A: He just flipped!

Every morning I plan on making pancakes,
but I keep waffling.

Q: What did the pancake learn in music class?
A: B-flat.

My daughter brought me breakfast in bed today—
scrambled eggs. They weren't all they were cracked
up to be.

Q: Did you hear about the haunted French pancakes?
A: They'll give you the crepes!

Did you know that milk is the fastest liquid on earth?
Yeah, it's pasteurized before you even see it.

Q: Which day do eggs hate?
A: Fry-day.

BREAKFAST

```
V I S N O F O P A K Y P I E P B H M L P
G W L T L I R W V G U F Z U M Q A K B K
H Z J C M V T A C J C L R V N G A O N R
H W A E E V J F B H P Y M Q B D Q W B G
G X C Z G R M F I N S G T G D F O E N C
J S K C O V F L O N I R Q G K N Y C S E
E E I R P T A E A M X E W U D B O I N J
B E H L X Q X S L O R E T S E L O H C Z
E O Y C U T F H I Q A B K O D Q I J G C
G N I I I I E O R N S G Y P R Z W Q Y P
G T L D W U Z X S R T K I F H P Z G E U
S E U N P R Q O P A T Z H A V R X M D I
S V Q K B F J A Z C Z G U J P O Y T C Z
Q N N F B Q R D L A H M D F C W X R L Y
Q H A S H B R O W N S V A N B S U U W T
S Y Y G J I X K D W Q K K I G O O G P E
R A I S I N B R A N D A D F O L E O C L
W V G L G B T T T O A S T F I V X Y W E
V I Z K B R Z R H S P C W U Y Y Q Q T M
V R G A E R Y A Q J Q A W M O M U K A O
```

CHILAQUILES	HASH BROWNS	RAISIN BRAN
CHOLESTEROL	MUFFIN	SYRUP
COLD PIZZA	OMELET	TOAST
EGGS	PROTEIN BAR	WAFFLES
FRUIT	QUICHE	YOGURT

Rusty shows up late for work. The boss approaches him as he walks in.

"You should've been here at 8:30!" he yells.

Rusty looks surprised. "Why? What happened at 8:30?"

Did you know that name-dropping at work is the worst thing you can do? My coworker Robert De Niro told me that.

Did I ever tell you I had a job smashing cans?
It was soda pressing.

Q: How is Christmas like another day at the office?
A: Because you do all the work and some fat guy in a suit gets all the credit!

I don't mind going to work every day—it's the sitting around for eight hours waiting to go home I can't stand.

To all the coworkers who have talked about me behind my back: You discussed me.

AT THE OFFICE

```
L E U B D N O Q E Q U N Q S B E G C W N
H L B J N V C P C T U X J H M R S U W Z
H L Z X T J N B N U V V L N O J F F A A
N E Q W D D B P E X Z C V M D Q H U C O
A B B L V I E A R Q M H X J N B Y A X F
B M T B Y G S T E E H S D A E R P S F H
Y V N M R I G X F X A X G M R X V S D D
X R Z A L S J L N D Y Z W C K S Y I W X
E C A J F M B E O B N P H Z T J Z S A X
H C N L Q G N W C X T G F R N V Q T C K
X P N Z A P N E G D A B I O S V M A P D
M E U A V S J O L X K A I O H S F N E X
D L A J N O L I X U S T J E C R D T M S
E H L J F I A C O F O M G W H E Z S P C
Q A R G Y M F X Z M Q V Y G C T Z E L A
Z F E S E C R U O S E R N A M U H S O R
O A V X T H K R L B T S D V O P B U Y P
Z F I B X K P Y R E G A N A M M P I E O
Y D E W W J O N Q V C W P C Q O M T E O
X P W A K W F R H Q F A F L U C B S S L
```

ANNUAL REVIEW CONFERENCE MANAGER
ASSISTANTS E-MAIL PROMOTION
BADGE EMPLOYEES SALARY
CARPOOL FINANCE SPREADSHEET
COMPUTERS HUMAN RESOURCES SUITS

Did you hear about the drummer whose girlfriend gave birth to twin daughters?
He named them Anna 1, Anna 2.

At the height of his career, Elvis was in a nightclub in Las Vegas having a drink when a fan approached him.

"Elvis, would you come by that table over there and say, 'Hey, how've you been?' to me?"

Elvis declined. "I'm just trying to relax here."

"Please? I'm a huge fan, and it would really impress my date."

Reluctantly, Elvis agreed. A few minutes later, he approached the table. "Hey! How've you been?" he asked.

"Elvis! Can't you see I'm busy?"

 @Kim_pulsive

Lorde wrote her Grammy nominated album at age 14. My son is 13 and has let the bathtub overflow twice while he was sitting INSIDE of it.

I never let my kid watch an orchestra on TV.
There's just too much sax and violins.

DAD'S FAVORITE TUNES

```
S N W W D W V B K D V W O J D M V E M Q
E L V I S O K S C W I R W C R N R E S S
L P O X Y I C I O H S A C H E I V Z N N
T F W X F W R Q R X G O T O T H A P R A
A J B F N A K G B L O J B B F U Z B N Z
E K X X D G G F J B C I F M G F X Y Z B
B C L I V Z I X Y O U H Z W U M U M B T
E S O W I O S T L C R T H P X Z O D F C
H V R P A A Z L J C P I P R N N L R H M
T Q Z P V N E E U Q H M P K I W D D F D
S W H G F C P H U M L S O Y D L O E Z N
X E U V T A A L I K W O N D E R B T U U
G T X I R A A M E C W R J Z D F D A O R
Z D O N G D N X C B F E K P F O S R Z M
Z N N Y J J J Y D V M A D T B E A J E E
J O E L F R B I M O L T S P X A J Z O O
T A N U Z O B E Z N B O Y U O U C E N R
Q J J A C K S O N B R K C Q Q J Y U X M
L P V V Q T T V J A W C B V A U Y L N P
M X S E N O T S G N I L L O R C F J P J
```

AEROSMITH	JACKSON	ROLLING STONES
CASH	MOTOWN	RUN-DMC
COLLECTION	QUEEN	THE BEATLES
DR. DRE	RADIO	VINYL
ELVIS	ROCK	WONDER

Q: What is the biggest difference between chemistry and cooking?
A: In chemistry, you should never lick the spoon.

Dad: Sorry, but I only know how to make two dishes: meat loaf and apple pie.
Kid: Which one is this?

My family went out for the afternoon, so I decided to cook them dinner as a special treat. But when they came home, the fire trucks ruined the surprise.

Q: What did the chef give his wife for Valentine's Day?
A: Hugs and quiches.

 @Death_Buddy

walks outside
Its real quiet.. Almost too quiet.
looks around
lights BBQ
*1000 Dads emerge from nowhere giving
generic BBQ advice*

KISS THE COOK

```
Z K Q Y R L L U Z G T W Q C Z Z W Q R M
E D E B A N M C T R C V O Y G P Z K B Q
I V L O I E Y O R X B A W A E X T S A I
N Q A C P T T X O Z K V Y D Z M B I R W
S O O I G P A E K O M S Y I G I Z A B Y
P L C X Q I E U A B K G C L W F C D E X
F E R F W M M N T S F D J O F L A B C S
R C A A Z S W S L O G M E H B O K B U D
Z G H C S J R B Z C S O G F I U L V E A
Q V C Y F P Y P H I U S D Y J R R T K J
Q C H A R R E D F A A O M Q C I H Y K T
W E S A P V I Y A L U P H X F P G I R Y
V B Z M F D B S V U P F R G G E F Q U D
K E E Y D Z X L W O Q Z E O S F R T A Q
V R S M C W K L H P E H M H N G U F W O
R W A N X Y S I F P X X I W C T D B A J
B R G P I T R R I Z G N P W N V H G C O
R F F A E V I G L I W S T Z U D A W Z W
V J A A R N P U L M E S X E R I X J V P
S B K Q K E I S L B J T Q Z P W S E A R
```

APRON

BARBECUE

CHARCOAL

CHARRED

CHEF

DRY RUB

GRILL

HOLIDAY

MEAT

PARK

RECIPE

SEAR

SMOKE

SOCIAL

STEAK

There was a robbery at the Apple Store today.
They caught the guy because they had an iWitness.

Q: What do you call a group of security guards in front of the Samsung store?
A: Guardians of the Galaxy.

Q: Who is the patron saint of e-mail?
A: St. Francis of a CC.

 @omgthatspunny

If you take a laptop computer for a run you could jog your memory.

Q: What does a young computer call its father?
A: Data.

Apple representative: Have you tested out the new iPhone?
Microsoft rep: No, actually, I haven't.
Apple rep: Neither have we!

TECH SAVVY

```
N V B M E T S O A I D J B J R G K A N C
X P I D Q C H D A Y K N N N Q H E E Z N
U O V R X G G V N T C Q H V M I H O Z K
U R G C A M G H F I W N G S N U O C G T
M M V A J L O N L F B E O Z R M J S I M
G U E V R G P X M S C Q R A I D E Q L H
S R P D Y W T H T D I W D N A B B V C Q
H T M L O N F O R J J P T H F H T X L Z
G D G R S M V F O F X I L Z D U G N G E
L R A T N B R I C B B E Q Q K E U M A K
U O R P O Y K H J G E D B L Z J B S U V
T O E C I K I D J N R R U P B D B I H X
X H W F T P Q J A O O B R Q X U Y Y Y C
P P Q I A K T Z W W A S Z N B C B I P X
U H W Z C U H S S Z U I W Y T V A V X Z
K Y H J I Z S E E T K T U T M S J C X D
N V F S L A R B B V C O O K I E W E H X
O F C J P G Z E D O L A L Q N E H I G E
O S I Z P F J M T B U F R B Z D O W F D
G S R M A Q I F O F B W B I M Y D W N I
```

APPLICATIONS	COOKIE	RE-BOOT
BANDWIDTH	HTML	VIRAL
BROWSER	IPAD	VPN
CACHE	MODEM	WI-FI
CHIP	PASSWORD	ZOOM

How many politicians does it take to change a lightbulb?
Two: one to change it and another one to change it back again.

————————————

Politicians and diapers should both be changed regularly… and for the same reason.

————————————

A thief sneaks up behind a man and sticks a pistol in his ribs. "Give me your money!"

The man, shocked by the attack, says, "You can't do that, I'm a United States congressman!"

The thief thinks for a moment and replies, "In that case, give me my money!"

————————————

Somebody threw a football at President Trump.
A Secret Service agent shouted, "Donald, duck!"

————————————

"I've been to war. I've raised twins. If I had a choice, I'd rather go to war."
–George W. Bush

POLITICS

```
K F E Q D R B D G U M K K R Q A I R H T
G K W S U O K S I F M K P K P V J W Q G
L S P O L I C Y E V Q P Q E E E C B B G
G J O R C U J W U C I R B L H L A I B H
E G D U J V X G G U A D V Q R E K G A Z
P W X F G N E G R U O N E L A O Y E B F
G R E E D G Q K A U K F D D E G O T D P
L K T D D E C I D E D M T I F W I A P R
F O D P H V C T V W P V E A D M E C O E
V L G Y L B P B C V T T K S A A X U A S
A A Z L B U R V J T V J B R D N T D T I
R T N L P T T T X B Y A M I S W P E D D
F C M E H J C Y X Q I E P H L C X F E E
L K Z P C Q Y T E S V K T L W L X H M N
J W D A R T B C W X L V G D M D S G O T
I O O O A O I Z O U G O B E I R L R C C
F V T J E T K I E O X S O C E U I D R I
K C O N S E R V A T I V E T T M V N A B
C Z G U E J B S L G I D U R O Z M P C B
D V J N R L B P K P V F L O D P C E Y U
```

ARGUE	DEMOCRACY	JUSTICE
BILLS	DIVIDED	POLICY
CANDIDATE	EDUCATE	PRESIDENT
CONSERVATIVE	GREED	RESEARCH
DECIDED	JUDGE	VOTE

Q: What time does Serena Williams wake up?
A: Ten-ish.

During the 1993 Super Bowl, the Buffalo Bills fumbled the ball on their own 45-yard line, where it was recovered by Dallas Cowboys lineman Leon Lett. He then did what few linemen ever do: He ran it all the way to the other end for a touchdown. As he was about to cross the goal line, he slowed down to celebrate, raising the ball in triumph…and it was knocked out of his hands by a Bills receiver hot on his tail. What a Lettdown.

Q: What do sprinters eat before a race?
A: Nothing. They fast.

Golf pro: Now I want you to go through the motions without actually hitting the ball.
Student: But that's what I always do!

Q: Why couldn't the Olympian listen to music?
A: Because he kept breaking all the records.

SPORTS ICONS

```
Z Z F H E K N A M L L I T B P S T C U G
V N S H G Q D R G S M R A Y W H R O S E
U Y E E Y R N R B M G P F P Z A P Y Y L
Z U U B I C E R X U G P C A J Q U N E M
A N I S A K Y T F Y B R E K N Z D I I Y
U P Z Y F B C S Z J M H S X F A K F E O
C Y E H P V F A Q K Y T X H B M Y R M Y
N A X O E A V A J N Y K E E P S B W U M
B Y Z I J F L M C L E W I S H S W E U A
C Z U D H D I I F Y P S E X K Q L Y K F
W H E O L P E R Z L D R S E R R W U N G
K D D Y E P M X G M Q E C L T A B D R D
F R Q L R P W R X V T Q N F I I B A U T
F V E O R L E Z L R K H M C K N G G Q X
Z C H A U I E A G P G G J L O X V E S J
X T W X Z G J V C B W F Q V Z B V X R U
C N F A C H P J C Q S B A H T E B R L B
Y U R V A T A N Q N O S L E K C I M R I
C F B S W A X Y Y V C K H N E S S Y E H
C L R T P N X S D V D I U K J U V C W U
```

ALI

BABE

COBB

FRAZIER

GRETZKY

JACKIE

JOEPA

LEWIS

MICKELSON

PELÉ

ROSE

SHAQ

THORPE

TIGER

TILLMAN

An archaeologist is the best husband a woman can have: the older she gets, the more interested he is in her.

Did you hear about the marble statue that left her husband? She was tired of being taken for granite.

I once gave my husband the silent treatment for an entire week, at the end of which he declared, "Hey, we've been getting along great lately!"

Therapist: So why do you want to end your marriage?
Her: I'm sick of all his Star Wars jokes.
Him: Divorce is strong with this one.

A father of five won a toy at a raffle. He called his kids together to ask which one should have the present.

"Who is the most obedient?" he asked. "Who never talks back to Mother? Who does everything she says?

Five small voices answered in unison, "Okay, Dad, you get the toy."

MARRIAGE

```
T R W D B W N B N V N M L N U Y U D N Y
K M G G H H C L V P R A X J A Z B L P S
G N U V A D K M L A E D I B T Y S T N A
H T Y B P N C M L D Y R W B D O T W Z Y
I Q G S P B Y D I D E K C V H F B P X T
G D F B Y H S V P Q B M J I K M Q T V P
V L T L Z M O A M Y O B V W O O Y A T T
N R B S L R G W N P O T D J L Q W K H S
H V H E P D W N W G W E U H U Z B E W U
A R E N T R A P I Q O R T M X C K N H R
C C T C S T P D P L E A E G G R O O M T
W Z X Z T N E A Z F E H D G Y Y Z W W G
I Y I W S K P R R H G S E H I V P H O C
E E H R R V W K H E E B N Y J R O R A F
D Y W U S E H L R A N W A U Y E R X V U
I W H I F E W T L G L T K W O I E Z O A
R U J I N T I M A C Y F S D Z C A X L G
B N W O H W V Q D I K R T S I P K I D C
W W A F I D D F L T H G I N E T A D H N
Q A K T Z N C L K Z S E I T P C U W F C
```

BETTER HALF	HAPPY	PROVIDE
BRIDE	INTIMACY	SHARE
COUNSELING	JOIN	TAKEN
DATE NIGHT	PARENTS	TRUST
GROOM	PARTNER	WIFE

I heard the new auto body shop in the neighborhood comes highly wreck-amended.

A mechanic called one of his customers after a check bounced. "The check you wrote to pay your bill came back!" he yelled.

The customer replied, "Well, so did all my car problems that you supposedly fixed!"

A set of jumper cables goes into a bar. "Can I get a drink?" the cables ask.

"Okay," the bartender replies. "But don't start anything."

REAL NOTE LEFT ON A CAR WINDSHIELD

"I hit your car, I'm sorry! Because you looked rich, I'm not leaving my number."

Did you hear about the driver who ran into a truck full of strawberries?
Talk about a traffic jam.

CAR REPAIR

```
P Z E S P X F C P C Q I W S T V M I Y B
C L T H E R M O S T A T Q C J E X D M L
U U J W A D S O B D F H Z K A T K N C L
X E J W K A O L C B P R W W N F J S C K
H E B O I I F A J K D G T K A E L O A U
H U K Q C H V N V M T N V S M L O B U G
S D G S Z B F T M X P I K I X Q Z J O Y
I P C K H E O L E S A R Q D U U V M N F
O W G J E Y L N Z Q B E B X S B S J V B
E Y K S K P I E V W X E R H P J L G Q H
M S H L G G A S M P Y T P H A R V L L A
S F R S N X P A U Y Y S Y I R W B Y M V
G D K E D A T B O S E F Q Y K D C E U R
S I I W P Y I P R Z W E D W P W K D L E
X I I X Z I P E B O B Q E E L T J E C T
Q N G Z X J W O O Y Q V N K U U G F H L
C Y K N A R Y Q F Z E T T N G X N N O I
P E R N A F X J O R O W G S M X B T R F
W M J F I L P P U D D U S B G Y K Z N P
W F G W Q J B L H P L B H J W H I I J M
```

BELT	GASKET	SMOG
COOLANT	HORN	SPARK PLUG
DENT	LEAK	STEERING
ENGINE	LUG NUT	THERMOSTAT
FILTER	SIGNAL	WIPERS

A man and his daughter were at the zoo. They were watching the tigers, and the father was talking about how ferocious they are.

"Daddy, if the tigers got out and ate you up—"

"Oh, honey, don't worry about that."

"—which bus would I take home?"

A kid presented her father with a drawing of Earth that she made in school. "Do you like it, Daddy?" she asked.

"Sweetie," he said, "this means the world to me."

Q: What's another name for twins?
A: Womb-mates.

Kid: In class, we're studying different people's names and where they came from. Why is my sister named Daisy?
Dad: Because your mom's a gardener and loves flowers.
Kid: Oh! Thanks.
Dad: You got it, Sleeping in the Hammock.

KIDS' NICKNAMES

```
T Y T D B O Y W U N M F E W A K M F W D
G A K E Y B Y Y O I Y T Q M C G Z X C C
C K R Z V V M Q U K H M J Y I A R R H U
H N E Q W L Q T T P U Y W J N N L L I P
T W I M N M Q M I M Q T O L S D I O C C
U N S I P L U I G U F V S N A V T M K A
T X H D E F L E X P U C R E T T U B A K
S X J U F B O C X U N W T T X S I K D E
T P I I N F C J F C K Z F V Q G T K E L
S W N E T T I K N Q L C Z Q L Z Y F E T
W U X Y W G T A O G T V D X P E W L S I
A A N H H H R N G F F F K S N Q O M X G
W M I S E J M G W T Y Q K O S L U C Y E
Q N L D H L Q E G B E T H W P Y W E K R
U R Y M J I D L C S C G M A W X A M J H
U N B T F C N O J P N A G T V T O F L A
H V U Z P I J E O V N S M U K P A A T Y
I R B U U U C H U N K Y M O N K E Y S T
Q O B S N J J L E H R J Y U C G I I H K
W C A B P L E U N S Y Z T E K T T E L I
```

ANGEL	CUPCAKE	NOODLE
BUBBA	HONEY	NUGGET
BUTTERCUP	KITTEN	PUMPKIN
CHICKADEE	MINI ME	SUNSHINE
CHUNKY MONKEY	MUFFIN	TIGER

Q: Why don't calculus majors party?
A: Because you can't drink and derive.

I'd tell you a chemistry joke, but I don't know if I'll get a reaction.

Kid: My math teacher said I'm average.
Parent: Well, that's just mean.

I studied abroad in college.
And then I asked her to marry me.

BAD ADVICE FROM A REAL DAD

"My dad (who has a bachelor's degree in finance) told me that you can use credit cards as free money as long as you pay the minimum payments."

My son didn't go to Harvard or Yale, but he's been to an I.V. league institution.

UNIVERSITY MAJORS

```
G U W O N S S E N I S U B X D S Y Z L G
U H N A O J C Q M Y W M J T Q A A C C Z
G G W Y L S O H P S C F L S G J R L D R
K E O Y G N L X D S I X L P W M R P E M
D K F D X O Q X W A Q L Q E A T I M S S
I I B N F I L F T Q M E A I N E Q G F N
Z I E C R T E O B T N F J N H I D O R Q
T V X M S A F S H Q P D O Z R V O N Y T
C R J I O C X E M C Q B Y J P U G G K Z
H B A E X I C H U R Y J Z J O X O R U X
I J Q S M N W W D Y X S V T C L F J U A
R F O L K U Q G G Y S I P S O L O H U R
O M Z A A M P O Z Z C Z Z I W C I N Y K
P K S P H M L X D P I F B A I S K U W B
R L D U T O C O J X M V T S T N V R J J
A V T S E C K H L E O N U O A I W S H V
C E M H E D O Z Q M N M R G F F W I N X
T O T L B Z G D L H O Y U I S P W N G X
I B G N I T N U O C C A J M I Y P G A M
C F D K L F S D X D E W I P B X H A A K
```

ACCOUNTING   ECONOMICS   MUSIC
BIOLOGY   FILM   NURSING
BUSINESS   HISTORY   PSYCHOLOGY
CHIROPRACTIC   JOURNALISM   SALES
COMMUNICATIONS   LAW   THEOLOGY

Q: What do you get if you cross a sheepdog with a rose?
A: A collie-flower.

———————

"I can see for miles," said Miles' guide dog.

———————

An aspiring veterinarian put himself through veterinary school working nights as a taxidermist. When he graduated, he decided he could combine the two occupations. On the door of his new business: "Dr. Boone, Veterinary Medicine and Taxidermy: Either way, you get your dog back!"

———————

Q: What happened when the dog ate the firefly?
A: It barked with de-light!

———————

My dog used to chase people on a scooter a lot. It got so bad we had to take his scooter away.

———————

Q: How is a dog like a phone?
A: It has collar ID.

MAN'S BEST FRIEND

```
H B E J D S P G R E A T D A N E D C A A
H G U W A N W Y P S U K U E N R P F C R
W H A G L R U A U B L Y Y B I G H O B L
F G U O M R U O C N C V I Z S L A X S D
R W O V A B M R H K F S Z V V K L H G S
Y I A E T L N R D D D K T M U V L O I N
J H A U I P Y C D M O F D B L V B U C K
V E T S A E I K H R L O H U E J Q N F P
R Z U P N U V Z Z Q J T L Y U R H D N V
X E S X N E H E K S I E L B X B N H G F
C O X P Q H X J Y R C M S B E K C A W O
N D B O J A E T N W N R Z V Q F D S R F
T P L C B Y N C N A U A Z S T M U T T D
J D M S P B T G A G M C H L S P L H E O
A T A G I M F K O Y G A A J X U U H V L
H E S U Y Y A V G D R X Y U C B M P R J
D S T M C G F N F P L N K O G B H U K X
E I I D E T C R E I T L S D J G Z G O L
W B F M M X K I D F F D U W N H I O D Y
P W F G I U H A G L D I H B R U M E F M
```

AUGGIE   DALMATIAN   MUTT
BLOODHOUND   FOXHOUND   PUG
BOXER   GREAT DANE   SHAR PEI
BULLDOG   HUSKY   ST. BERNARD
COLLIE   MASTIFF   VIZSLA

"There is no sunrise so beautiful that it is worth
waking me up to see it."
–Mindy Kaling

FROM A COMEDY ROUTINE BY GEORGE BURNS AND GRACIE ALLEN:

George: Gracie, what day is it today?
Gracie: Well, I don't know.
George: You can find out if you look at that paper on your desk.
Gracie: Oh, George, that doesn't help. It's yesterday's paper.

"When my kids become wild and unruly, I use a nice
safe playpen. When they're finished, I climb out."
–Erma Bombeck

Did you hear about the clown who lived in
the desert?
He had a dry sense of humor.

FUNNY FOLKS

```
Q X R B E G D L G H O W J Q W O O T Z K
E R O Y R P R Z E Y L P L P J N S T E E
A L V L C I P H F U B E R N I E M A C H
G N L A V S U L X E V Q E O M R O Q X Q
X E T E M B F E B O T T D B F K J O C V
N D R B N S T Z M V C K D E A W N Y O Z
J S I V T C I B U R J S F N X J B N S L
O T E Z A H M I Q D X X O Y W Y Q D B B
P G C T T I X P E Z E F X C E Z V V Y Y
B E A Z M Y S N D A W L X I L B S P R H
X G A L V Y W D O F N B L Q W B P O V U
Z U B M I I O A H S L I J E P P T G O O
N N D U E F A A D Q N T T L P R N R X C
C V R L P I I B U H S I E R G P A N Y O
S L F C E M O A Q A F I K P A I A R B J
X E X P A F E D N K L Y F T U M F H T W
H O K A V R N D Q A L J X O A Q B V C T
G L M Y Z S L I X P K N J N I Z T T Q C
G F R X S E D I E E N I N O Y Y N Q J P
S R U I R X Q J N S S X S B S K Q S B F
```

ATKINSON

BERNIE MAC

CARLIN

CHAPPELLE

COSBY

ELLEN

GALIFIANAKIS

GERVAIS

MARTIN

PRYOR

REDD FOXX

RIVERS

SANDLER

SEINFELD

SYKES

Q: What are the four worst words you can hear on a golf course?
A: "It's still your turn."

I got excited when my son joined the cross-country team. But then I learned they don't cross the country and they're back home in just a few hours.

Q: How do snowboarders introduce themselves?
A: "Sorry, dude!"

There are two seasons in Canada: winter, and poor snowmobiling season.

What's the difference between a baseball hitter and a skydiver?

The baseball player goes "smack!...ARGH!" A skydiver goes "ARGH!...smack!"

THE WORLD OF SPORTS

```
F Y C O T S B I H Q J A N J W A B E Y T
C S C G E U Z F O A B Y C T E S P U P S
W O T G A W U R J K N O G L C A V Q C J
U P G L M M R Q O Y S T A T I S T I C S
V V P U S D E H P S O H G X Z W A J I C
S I D Z J D W C B M T Z D R J A G C L L
J J V E D P N Q S P B E S W S W S I O U
A F D C O X T R T S K G R I L P Z O N L
S C R R L I E S X P N B S R A N K E D K
Y H P O R T E Z N M L E O O K T S M V W
V Z I F R E C B D O F X S L T Y P L A Y
O I G A R A N U O P I G U Q J F V S E C
F B T E G A X Q E P W T L R C V C D K Q
U S F X G S F L F B L C C K S O C Q W W
O E F A N S U B D Z D A A I R T Q Q M I
R B K P I D Q T G F Y Q T E D V X C K N
H M J U E H R C H S V V K R D E S O X J
J P X H L U U S L N W G S P H P R F B U
C W C A R R W W T O D N I S E S G P O R
U S L P O S I T I O N F N E T H Y Q S Y
```

FANS   RANKED   STARTERS
INJURY   REFEREE   STATISTICS
PLAY   ROSTER   TEAMS
POSITION   SCHEDULE   TROPHY
PREDICTIONS   SCORE   UPSET

Kid: Dad, how much does it cost to get married?
Dad: I don't know. I'm still paying for it.

 @ConanOBrien

Just taught my kids about taxes by eating 38% of their ice cream.

Pride is what you feel when your kids net $100 from a garage sale.
Panic is what you feel when you realize your car is missing.

"I believe that we parents must encourage our children to become educated, so they can get into a good college that we cannot afford."
–Dave Barry

I always carry a picture of my family in my wallet. It's a reminder of why there's no money in my wallet.

I thought your mom's wedding ring was expensive. Think of how much Saturn's must have cost.

MAJOR EXPENSES

```
A K A F K S A R V C D M F Z V Y U A P J
X D Z I B W G A C E J A A C K E J N L P
L T V Y R F Z D B Y Z N A N O B I D A O
E H D Z R F U T H A I R O L A N R L Z Z
X P F O I F A T F O S P I D X Y L Q D N
I L L O C I H R O K U A O U E C S X P N
B E A C R T W S E C E S P R H P G F O O
X X J K A T X U E D K K E P L S U J U I
W O Q O Q O E N I S U O M I L N Z P I T
J B B Y I Z D U E A I Y B A E E C I Y A
S S V O G T U I S U A M N R T X X A Q C
T G M P O V C Q I E C N A R U S N I Q A
P S F C N K A N U H Q L D M K X X R H V
A G R N W Y T K R J M R J K L B S Y S C
G A G U W Q I Q C A A E W L Q B Z Y A N
Q K P Y R F O K P B R M W D F I H B R U
O F V Q L X N R R W B F M K V O L X F O
R H T G P O Q T C G Y U C S P F U G M K
Q W A S L O O T R E W O P Q F Z W P I V
N G E Q L A Y O A M J C X T I Q W K Q F
```

AIRFARE

APPLE

BOAT

CARS

CRUISE

DEBT

DRYER

EDUCATION

FUNERAL

HOUSE

INSURANCE

LIMOUSINE

POWER TOOLS

ROLEX

VACATION

Wife: I thought we agreed on three beers and be home by ten.

Husband: I'm sorry, honey, I always get those two mixed up.

A couple sits on the porch, watching the sunset, each with a beer in hand. The husband says, "I love you so much."

The wife says, "I love you, too. But is that you or the beer talking?"

The husband answers, "It's me, talking to my beer."

Sometimes I'll open a root beer and it fizzes so loudly that it sounds like it's talking to me.

You know, soda speak.

Knock-knock!

Who's there?

A magically refilling glass of beer.

Well, come on in!

Three soldiers in training headed into town and got too drunk at a bar. They knew they were off base.

HAVE A COLD ONE

```
W A K C N F M J T W T A G P S Y P E P G
R U E W M P O E R F L N F A D E C V G W
L K I U L L T A H E A M U L Z M Q Q V J
T T H U P K E M Z L M R Y E F Z B T O T
T D S I D S N S J N G J C A W Y S N Q G
S O N A E C V C N S E A R L O P V J A B
R S N Y E T T H E I C X N E O K V V N O
K E T L I Y I A N P A G H H L Y Z Q U S
T Q Q W T I R L O C I R G N P L Z A I Q
M U Q K M P D N R N B M G J Z H A X U E
A I G S D Q S T E E L R E S E R V E I L
M S C J O G X T J U L C N F C J G N K H
D C Q H R Y Q T S W J L Z Q C R O T M B
W L Y V E R P B H M M A I L V O Y V G B
E I O O C L K W G A N T B M M U J T Z N
R J T C Z B O J M B A G Y E L S M K C E
B L W B O Z R B O Q X Z U H U N U H M M
B F I C I R S F O G I L U G K M N X H P
M G I W P E B M N B B R J G Z L A G E R
I U X U H A R B P T L S C P G V V O Y V
```

BLUE MOON	GRAINS	MILLER LITE
BREW	HOPS	PALE ALE
COLD	LAGER	STEEL RESERVE
CRAFT	MALT	WITBIER
DOS EQUIS	MICHELOB	YEAST

Kid: Dad, can you teach me how to play chess?
Dad: Sure, let me pick up a board at the pawn shop.

I was having dinner with Bobby Fischer over a checkered tablecloth. It took him two hours to pass the salt.

 @iwearaonesie

watching the kids play hide and seek in the park and mine just hid behind a chain link fence

at least we don't have to save for college

I don't play hacky sack to look cool.
I do it just for kicks.

My mother was extremely overprotective. As kids, we were allowed to play "Rock, Paper, Paper."

Q: How do astronauts pass the time?
A: They play Moonopoly.

FUN AND GAMES

```
Q S M Y P N C L U S A T A W G C D X R Y
Y B Z V X G S L S Y T U D F O L L A C E
J O I R A M R E P U S G F C K A Y O Q C
T T A H I I E D T M L U U Y U S A P K A
N L J C I N K W G I Q W Y E B L I E M J
Q R I S J E C U B D R R P C S W E R M B
F U O R I C E I E F S D T Y T S O P I V
Z O Q W S R H P D R Y H D Z D E W K X V
Z F K L B A C F B L U L P N A G T H H C
K T V M G F B F Y A B H A E M Q P R O C
K C C W Y T R X L P O E L U R U G C I N
T E A H N A M C A P D X O L M A K F V S
K N R N M X R Z S I D Q V C X J V W G P
M N L R D V G C H C W L P A E X V O B X
U O U V Q Y O U G X H X R Z X M L W G C
W C D Y Z T L Y A Z P S R J T F Q G Y W
Q T M Q C T N A U Q F O P L N P V B R M
T P S H C T T M N D A R R Z D Z H C F S
Q K B X A Z H Y Q D K R N I P I Y C A J
N J W G W Y O S A G Z Y D Q I J G P F K
```

CALL OF DUTY	GUESS WHO?	RISK
CANDY LAND	HIDE-AND-SEEK	SORRY!
CHECKERS	HOPSCOTCH	SUPER MARIO
CLUE	MINECRAFT	TAG
CONNECT FOUR	PAC-MAN	TETRIS

Q: Which rock group has four men who can't sing?
A: Mount Rushmore.

BUMPER STICKER:

TV Is Gooder Than Books

My wife is really mad that I have no sense of direction. She picked a big fight with me after we got lost in a bad neighborhood. That was the last straw. I packed up my stuff and right.

VANITY LICENSE PLATES

ITSYELLO (on a yellow car)
NOT COP (on a Crown Victoria)
OJ DID IT (on a white Ford Bronco)
NOT-POOR (on a Mercedes)
SORRY (on a car with Canadian plates)
SHELEFT (on a sports car)

FAMILY ROAD TRIP

```
F T K D W S U U O O N O N K E I U N R J
H D X Z D B O K E L Y Q V V K D Z E G R
N G Z S L K O W Q Y I K W C W Z M W O E
Z L Z E E D O G E W X V K P L C O W O S
I I C M U R V D O A B E Z S C E B R Q T
H B S N O I T I D E P X E Q I C M W Y S
T Z H D M G L X J I M T Y S Z L U C T
Z S K N V T E P V Y M B W M U T A D G O
P K N I S A E M Y G A Q V N M L S H L P
T Q S V X R K X C B L G N O P I R T Z B
H I S T I V O P W T J N R I X T L O L W
T K W E F M I E A G A M E S B G F L G P
Z X N L X R K A T S E U Q R F N T I A H
L C U A I F M H O M S Q R U P E T R L P
E C N R Y W O W D V C A R C P S H Z E Q
X Z I C V N S Z A T E W G X A D H B K K
C D P R Q Q Q T N X A Q D E T M W B D Y
E V S B V J H E O W L I O T X Y D K G A
I U K B L P F E W U E W E T K G X K U W
D A P R U X V O P Q R L H O H T A G J Q
```

EXCURSION   MUSIC   SPIN
EXPEDITION   PASSAGE   TOUR
EXPERIENCE   QUEST   TREK
GAMES   REST STOP   TRIP
LIFT   RIDE   VISIT

It's Game 7 of the NBA Finals, and a man makes his way to his seat at center court. He sits down and notices that the seat next to him is empty. He leans over and asks his neighbor if someone is sitting there.

The man responds, "No, the seat's empty."

The first man exclaims, "What?! Who in their right mind would have a seat like this for the NBA Finals and not use it?"

The neighbor responds, "Well, the seat is mine, but my wife passed away and this is the first NBA Finals we haven't been together."

"I'm sorry to hear that. Wasn't there anyone else, a friend or relative, who could've taken that seat?"

"No, they're all at the funeral."

Q: Why did the basketball player sit on the sideline and sketch pictures of turkeys?
A: He was trying to draw fowls.

Q: What kind of earrings do basketball players wear?
A: Hoops.

Basketball players are always so well-rested. You see, taller people sleep longer.

BASKETBALL PLAYERS

```
A M U R R A Y M Q B W P X L G T L E U O
R I A E K C R K P P L C X S C N D T C Y
W Q J L M O V C M M S W H I J M E L P E
I H V X O S O J O R D A N H L H R I D M
E T F U N N Q R F F Q D A W G N P W U F
B Z A F X U E H B Q Z F S A V P A G X Y
U C M B B W W T Y T M D H K E J K O D N
T B H N R S I A Z O S U R N E M D U O D
D G M U K P H K Z G C E O O D X N S A S
T A I D X L N W D Z W T W M I Z P L J B
A X V T L L Y E J F H W L U C M O X Z X
Q F B I B H D F R P N V S P O R Z C C C
K E H O S T N X I G U L Q H K X J B U F
M W B S Q B A Y O F R Z T R I Y H L R Z
X K B J O R U G D O R E G Q Z K L Y R S
Q Z V R T X V U P D H K V Q J F N Q Y G
F D N X K M P S S X A D X A B A Q K N R
S G H N L X V Z O R U S S E L L E D Y N
Q O E U A K A R E E M J Y L M C K J I F
A Z T C Y B D P A N S T U H G N O J R A
```

CURRY	KAWHI	PIPPEN
DAVIS	KLAY	RUSSELL
HILL	MALONE	THOMPSON
JORDAN	MURRAY	WESTBROOK
KAREEM	NASH	WILT

Q: How does Davey Crockett like his pie?
A: Alamo-d.

 @BoobsRadley

I bet the worst part of dating a documentary filmmaker is when he brings up things you did in the past and sets them to banjo music.

Kid: What's on TV?
Dad: Dust.

Q: How do you search for Will Smith in the snow?
A: Look for fresh prints!

Steve Harvey got in an argument with his father.
It was a Family Feud.

 @HomeWithPeanut

I feel you Oscar the Grouch. If I had to deal with that many kids all the time, I would hide in a trash can as well.

POPULAR TV SHOWS

```
U D S H S A M Z S C M Q R W H I F P Y L
D Q G L D V Z M Y D H Z E P W O O X A W
X B N R E I S A R F N A P N X I R Z D C
Z V I H U H K N Y I T E P S X P A X I G
A T W X J E P F T V D O I P Q Y A B F W
H W L Z X H A A T X S Q L R Y V P O L D
H Z N O F M K Q G W Q B F W F D B P W L
R Y N U Q F M C L P U H A J Y J A F P E
T G H O E V I F I I A W A H Q A D Y M F
X A G B W G F F F R A R Y U U M U O S N
D Z X V V G U K C Z E Z I I Y C L B T I
A T E I E P A N A T M X K Q T H Y G Y E
O S G S S M O W S X A O D H K Z A L H S
I C Y A U W O B X M E M E E C H B O I L
Q D C L O U E E L S O O A I Q N J Q J N
L N H L H W X N U R F K R A I R M V N Y
R N I A L P J W X F Z A E I E D Z I W C
Y T P D L D X Z I G M V P X G X C V K A
P S S U U X O C B F H E L Z R S R K U S
V I K S F I E O S P J Z M K P F F X C P
```

CHIPS

DALLAS

FLIPPER

FRASIER

FRIENDS

FULL HOUSE

GUNSMOKE

HAPPY DAYS

HAWAII FIVE-O

M*A*S*H

SEINFELD

TAXI

THE OFFICE

WEBSTER

WINGS

Did you hear about the shipload of paint that wrecked and marooned all the sailors?

A captain harpooned a whale's tail on his first throw. He said, "Well, that was a fluke."

First Mate: Feeding the prisoners to the sharks isn't any fun.
Captain: It is for the sharks!

Q: What do pirates snack on when they're at sea?
A: Swordines.

Did you hear about the sad cruise ship?
It was a woe boat.

Q: What do bald sea captains worry about?
A: Cap sizes.

SEAFARER

```
C G G M R E R J R J K K A I E E S I E N
T U X H E P C O F B Z R F B Q F N M M S
T Z Y S P U C W K W M J Q C D G T J P K
R O K C P M H K R L J P W F J V T E E S
H V O A I X R S E E F E N I G N E B S W
D B V R L Q B T H I I M Q K Y D T N L R
L A E E C Y X C L P A R P E D A A J Q Z
G X R S H L A U N C H F R T U B L H K H
A M B I P B U L K H E A D A T S Z W Z K
M E O U Y P N V H I U B G G C N J N B L
C Z A R C R O H C N A L K I L O M T W D
V V R C L D N C W T G C L V P J C I O L
S B D B B O X F T L S A F A O W I L F U
S Q V E I I G L V F A R C N K L D O C K
E K Q W C P E M O M D G Y N R H V D A F
X U R E K S P E Y S O O U X B K J Z J A
C T O E H O X J X T L S W X P C Z M B N
G A A I P K F Z Z K E H V L G Y H Z O H
K O P F T X A N L G C I N M I N G N R H
B J X V T Y K V N P F P E Q M N Z I X O
```

ANCHOR	CLIPPER	LAUNCH
BATTLESHIP	CRUISER	NAVIGATE
BULKHEAD	DOCK	OVERBOARD
CARGO SHIP	ENGINE	SPEED
CARRIER	HULL	TUG

"I just bought a new house. It has no plumbing.
It's un-can-ny."
–Morey Amsterdam

My grandfather was an honorable, brave man. He had the heart of a lion, and a lifetime ban from the zoo.

Q: When's the best time to go skydiving?
A: Fall.

REAL NOTE LEFT ON A CAR WINDSHIELD

"The next time you park here & block me in I will monster truck your car into a pile of scrap."

 @HenpeckedHal

Crossing your fingers can symbolize telling a lie or praying for divine intervention.
Either way, it perfectly sums up my parenting style.

RISK-TAKER

```
E Q T N E D I F N O C D W O A C X S O D
U B L W J E S B D K V V T N R T C J R K
S C G H T E V G P Z W E P J R N I U A B
R S Z Q L C J I X H R L R U P U Z A U X
U E E P O V S J T F H F D C N H R D O Y
P K M G X T H P I A E G B B O K S A E W
F Q C V Y C O P X E E A D D U M D P T E
Y T I L I B I X E L F R R M M N E T D M
A E A P R X X L P R I A C L E D P A Z C
N S E Z R O J Z F J G K Y M E P J B H K
W L D D I L T E I M Z T I Q H S X I X N
H I T W G V L U P N J U O K H P S L K O
G S T A N D O U T O B V Y Y V W K I M E
D U D P C M A D V E N T U R O U S T R I
B C V A K J V R D V K U A Y H V G Y J M
M C C G D H W X I T S W F B J I L G M J
X E H B Q V T R C N J E D M R A V B R E
I S A D B I U Y W T G V Z X E M Q N R P
N S S K H V E Z J V D H A Z F M K M W Q
A K E D V V G O Y B Q K A B Y D S Q A C
```

ADAPTABILITY   DARING   PURSUE
ADVENTUROUS   FEARLESS   STAND OUT
CHASE   FLEXIBILITY   SUCCESS
CONFIDENT   HUNT   TRUDGE
CREATIVE   OVERCOME   ZEAL

Q: What's the difference between a high-hit baseball and a maggot's father?
A: One's a pop fly. The other's a fly pop.

A father and his young daughter are outside Yankee Stadium, and the girl asks for a T-shirt that says "Red Sox Suck." The dad hesitates, but says, "You can have the shirt if you promise never to say those words."

"That's right," says the vendor. "Suck isn't a very nice word."

"No," replies the father. "I meant the words Red Sox."

Kid: What do you do when you get thirsty at a baseball game?
Uncle: Ask for a pitcher.

I love sports analogies.
They're a home run!

Q: What do baseball players wear on their knees?
A: Kneecaps.

"TAKE ME OUT TO THE BALLGAME"

```
S K C A N S F Y Q N N G J J S V M N D U
F O Z B V Y D K T P H D U I P U I L C W
O M O E W R J J A Z L Z J G Q Q E R N V
P T T Q Z K H O W D U G O U T I A B W B
S Z S X G V Z M R S W N L V F C M Q A V
E O B O N H D V Q K R S F Y K G G S X N
N M F J T V P E J I E B Q E N S E W R N
D P O A R E M A C G I Z R K S B J L L U
U V B D N K V J R Y O J O E A E Y P L X
L C B P U S I O W G A Y P L A G I I W J
A X M A U R D Q T C O F L U U R H G Z D
N K N F M I R S K R T T S U T Q S P T X
P U W P V N Y S M P I O U R A N C Z M B
H L R J U E B U F N C S P A E W M P Q G
G M G E J V W J B N K E V N S Z B E A Q
M L M B M U F O W R T A R E N A R N X G
M Y B T E O V W I C Q T R S W U G N A I
Q D S F N S H K O O X B L Y I E R A Z Q
A D Z B M P P L U M I A I V L D W N D A
Z M U E S S O L O C U F C G W P B T Z L
```

ANGEL	COLOSSEUM	HOME RUN
ARENA	CRACKER JACKS	PENNANT
AUTOGRAPH	DOME	PETCO
BASEBALL	DUGOUT	SNACKS
CAMERA	FIELD	SOUVENIRS

A little girl notices some strands of her mother's hair are turning white. "Mom," she asks, "Why is your hair turning white?"

Annoyed, her mother responds, "Because I have a little girl who is constantly making trouble and causing me to worry."

The little girl thinks about it for a few minutes and says, "So why is Grandma's hair all white?"

When I want to call a family meeting, I just turn off the WiFi and wait for them all to gather.

Q: What's the difference between a mom and a dad?
A: If you've got a nasty allergic reaction, Mom will want to take you to the hospital. Dad will wait and see because he doesn't want to make any rash decisions.

Son: Was I adopted?
Parent: Not yet, but we're still holding out hope.

Q: How do you make antifreeze?
A: Steal her snow pants while they're drying by the fire.

FAMILY TREE

```
Y I X I D V X R V O M P L L S E S R G P
X U G X W J N J R P Z N T Y I A I R Q L
Z Z C E A R N P Z A A T G U S Q O A A G
N Y H B N M Z A N R D L N P T B I G R X
T B L E B E A V G E Y M S H E J H O J C
Z A N F U W A W C N T T I M R D O V Q E
Q B H E Z S S L G T W O M X S M Z O Q L
T I L B R M Y M O T H E R F E L C N U M
F X O D V C E S V G R E K M N U J F H E
X D N X B C W E J I Y J Y I V C H E H E
X X F N I N C E Q X I D T C O T G V L Q
A R B O Y W J I C P I H S N I K A O T P
C S N O S G R B G O R B N A F U X L J S
S P H J Q F W B J L S E F O F E C E I N
H P K A E K B Q Y D C X E T N N X G R E
M L I G N N E L L T M M E G C K K B X C
A X U E T M Q I I H J T A N B S X X H B
C K T Q O V H O H F H G J O Q Y E A J D
M A P K P C N T B P E A D G Q L A S D V
Q C I O P G I M G D X F K D K G K R W O
```

BABY   GENEALOGY   NIECE

CHILD   GROOM   PARENT

CONNECTION   KINSHIP   SISTER

ENGAGED   LOVE   SONS

FAITHFUL   MOTHER   UNCLE

"Dad, will the pizza be long?"
"No, it will probably be round."

Being a parent means knowing how to unwrap a candy bar without making any noise.

Son: What does bargain mean?
Dad: Well, it means a great deal, actually…

I sent ten of these jokes to ten of my friends, hoping that at least one would make somebody laugh.
No pun in ten did.

"Remember: what dad really wants is a nap. Really."
–Dave Barry

I was playing a regular game of baseball with my dad.
Until he threw me a curveball.

Kid: Dad, do you have a sweet tooth?
Dad: Nope. I've got a whole mouth full!

THINGS DADS LIKE

```
S W P V U H O O J J Z F I R H W M R H F
G N M V F I F D H Q U F S J H I I B K W
S G E F E P B B Q A R L V U E Y A R J J
R F B V B Y O X S F Q O J L V V D J S O
B F C X R T D L X P M G Q R G Y F Y O B
H F Z U I O O S Q V S U C C F T O F D H
V Q M M A E Y P L G G N I H G U A L S Y
G Y Y M C Y N L E Q R S C W R N V C U U
T F L E X I N G N D T N Q O D Z Y Q C P
R O O Z Q H K A O E E C M H V C F A Z G
L O S D I K D N A R G M W V X U H I N S
R G D W X O I K G I K K O U X S H E D X
I G W I E S S R E L L I R H T O D E E T
C N V Y N A C M N W D D Y X S Z P P R H
B I F B O N T J I X I G B M U Z Y B S K
O E V P K C E S P Z L C T I W D E K F I
N B K Z W H Q R Y J N M I E K E C C L X
T S H I R T S L G H H P X X R A F K G S
R A C Q U E T B A L L M Y T N C K W C V
T R U K L B L O B R J O K S P A N J E I
```

BEER	GRANDKIDS	SNACKS
BEING GOOFY	HOME DEPOT	STEAK
DINNER	LAUGHING	SWEATS
FLEXING	NAPS	THRILLERS
GOLF	RACQUETBALL	T-SHIRTS

A lady was expecting the plumber at ten o'clock. Ten o'clock came and went; no plumber. Eleven o'clock, twelve o'clock, even one o'clock rolled around, still no plumber. She concluded he wasn't coming, and left to do some errands.

While she was out, the plumber knocked on the door. Her parrot, which was in a cage by the door, said, "Who is it?"

"It's the plumber."

He thought it was the lady who had said, "Who is it?" and waited for her to let him in. When this didn't happen, he knocked again, and again the parrot said, "Who is it?"

"It's the plumber!"

Still no one answered the door. He pounded on the door, and the parrot repeated, "Who is it?"

"It's the plumber!" he said, irritated.

Again, he waited; again, she didn't come; again, he pounded; again, the parrot said, "Who is it?"

"AHHHH!" he said, flying into a rage. He kicked the door in. He suffered a heart attack and fell dead in the doorway.

The lady came home from her errands, only to see the door ripped off its hinges and a corpse lying in the doorway. "A dead body!" she exclaimed. "Who is it?"

"It's the plumber!" the parrot answered.

MR. FIX IT

```
T W H K T P V W H K T X W A U X S Z U Z
H X B V S R Y A U Z E X O R R K Y U U T
G H M B G T I S A I G F U N O Y H B Y P
L N A M S T F A R C D I A J S H S O S H
L K M L W F L D G M F I J T R O J X S M
L G T U Y W K V X V L W D R Z E H Z L Q
N Q A S F B Q T M S M R J K G H X L K B
G Z C C I P R O F E S S I O N A L S V V
C Z T Y L L O I C Y E J X R K J S H L C
T Z H D Y K A B N A S I T R A G V I M G
H O E E Y U Z I Q W P F B C O U U S U O
H A Q I U A T F C H I M D T E O B I V C
B H A I B C X C L E T B M W W J H G W J
Y O U B J R W Q O E P I G D M G O J C C
J O D Y E N O H O A K S M U R V C R H Z
L G W F R A S A B C C X F S R I C R P Y
A M U Y E B W R S E E X F R Z U L X H R
O K O W C G B R E K A M M S B Q C L S H
V V S M B O B X G U C O N T R A C T O R
S E R V I C E E I I Q C K U V J X Z M F
```

ACE	GURU	PROJECT
ARTISAN	HONEY-DO	SAW
CONTRACTOR	MAKER	SERVICE
CRAFTSMAN	NAILS	SMITH
DRILL	PROFESSIONAL	SPECIALIST

Q: Why do trees hate tests?
A: The questions always stump them.

A woman hands her husband two kayak paddles.
"Which one do you want?" she asks.
   He replies, "Either oar."

Q: Where do saplings go to learn?
A: Elementree school.

Dad: You know, I can chop a log just by looking at it.
Kid: No way!
Dad: I'm serious. I saw it with my own eyes.

Q: What do baby bears eat?
A: Cub sandwiches.

Q: What happened to the camper who came down
with Lyme disease?
A: He got really ticked off.

CAMPING TRIP

```
H V G L W W V D X S J D I F S X G H D M
J H X C K H N I Q W F H Y N E B J J N C
Q X P S P D O G I E K J Q N K C B L X R
U O Z Y Q Z A Z G S D I C C A P W I E F
I C L V H Y B E S H Z C Z P L D Z A J I
Y Q Z E E W A R Q E C E D V M D J R O B
M E G I S R O W W N U E Y M K B K T I O
L V E N F O R O X P V G A M Q C E Z N C
V N S S D H A O C I I S I R H A H R S L
T P S T O O B D V H B H H B T M Q P E S
E R U T N E V D A H W N C C W P S G C O
K O R U U R L Y G B E J B K P G Y K T K
I F F R W K K V V T M Z P X Q R G E S H
Q X B C W Y I U L P R I C O W O F W A E
P Y A F K Q T F S W B G L Y H U U T Z O
P D N N Q X S M C Z S H Z C J N W W G V
K C H G T W E J O Y H J C C S D T Z N R
K J C T J X R E S F L A S H L I G H T Y
L B I U G I O A D D T C N Y J H B Z O H
S C E E R I F P M A C A T E N T G I E J
```

ADVENTURE   FLASHLIGHT   LAKE

BOOTS   FOREST   OUTDOORS

CAMPFIRE   GEAR   TENT

CAMPGROUND   HAT   TRAIL

CLIMB   INSECTS   WOOD

Q: When does a joke become a dad joke?
A: When the punch line becomes apparent.

Kid: Why did the chicken cross the road?
Dad: I don't know, ask your mother.

I had a good dad.
Or at least he was a better dad than his jokes were.

Q: What makes a kid laugh hardest at your dad jokes?
A: When she needs 20 bucks.

Daughter: Dad, why is there a "4" candle on the cake? I'm turning 15.
Dad: It's the only candle I had, so it's 4 your birthday.

Q: Why do dads tell dad jokes?
A: Because grandpa jokes fell asleep on the couch.

A dad pushed a tack into the wall. Standing below it, he called, "Hey, kids, c'mere!" When they gathered, he cried out, "Help me, I'm under a tack!"

HOW KIDS FEEL ABOUT DAD JOKES

```
D A R Z Y Y P D C P I N C C P O R Y L H
V T X R B J C I Y D E Y E F G Y E I E U
B L U S H S V S N Q E H U Y Q M V B E P
X M T U T U H B D E S A C X M V E X J O
P W M U B I Y E O O M S O H T M L S A J
X O P M V R O L F S B B P I B K C F A X
R I K N G P J I Q C U S A N L K U U V R
D V H S R R V E H X M O W R T W T Y G V
E G L I E L U F B T G Q I A R K M E T H
E J L W N Q N J M W I H F R S A D B D W
T Q H U Y Y E T M L R H E U A I S Z D P
I E A V O M Y S P A H E O O H L X S R A
R K T K Y S Y D G I O L T N X E I A E L
O V L X P N F F U Z U U P H C S Z H A D
V C D C R R L H O C L N T V G Q T Z M B
A O U O U U C U I N P J K K M U E Q H K
F H C Q C O V D Q T X Y B U S S A M O R
U L C W K Z I H H B J K T U G V F L S F
G R O A N R Q G Q F Y L L I S M W K P R
E B Q P S L P A N N O Y E D E G U Z H O
```

ANNOYED   EMBARRASSED   HUMOR
BLUSH   FAVORITE   LAUGHTER
CLEVER   GROAN   RIDICULOUS
CORNY   HIDE   SILLY
DISBELIEF   HILARIOUS   STUPID

Yesterday I asked my wife what she wanted for her upcoming birthday. She told me she wants something with a lot of diamonds. I sure hope she likes the deck of cards I bought her.

Q: When do sailors stop playing cards?
A: When their captain is on deck.

Did you hear about the fisherman magician?
He says, "Pick a cod, any cod!"

---

90 PERCENT OF PARENTING IS...

- Watching when someone says "watch this!"
- Pretending to be asleep.
- Shuttling kids to and from public bathrooms.
- Letting kids play games on your phone.
- Being late for things.
- Collecting box tops.
- Filling out permission slips.

Q: What's a good name for a woman who set her credit card bill on fire?
A: Bernadette.

DEALT CARDS

```
A E K Y J B R V N Q E Y S W U Z U P I A
F P K D J U D H C K K T N E D I S E R P
H F S Y H L N W C T R U M M Y B M Z P K
S B A W J P Z A I T V J M U C R R T E J
B D K P M Q X Z Y W I T V T L K F Z Q C
M V B V O R A X G X H P K U Y Q Y S H D
H M H G O C T Q C R N I X Z C G F N F J
Y D Q P U R S K D M B W S N M X H K P F
H C X D P M K G Q K G G Q T U Y T S U C
E T W Z F V C S B K Y P A Z Q Y J V B E
A C T V Y O A U N B J K G J J N V B O H
R O U O N U J R B O S D Z S H O E M A M
T W P R E R K K R M O W F C H E A T P W
S Q A R T J C M D N E P C P C R T P H S
K S O D D E A Y B X R H S B F Y N R G Z
X O A Y D D L V Y J E I O A B F B L O T
K G I J W Z B U C I Y K C O J S N D Z F
V W B R I D G E F M O N T H J W H D C Y
T W O Z U Q H U B P L O J F W H R M A O
C Q O W X K U Q O H L H X G T S M V O N
```

BLACKJACK	LE TRUC	RUMMY
BRIDGE	MAO	SCOPA
CHEAT	PITCH	SKAT
HEARTS	PRESIDENT	SPOONS
JASS	ROOK	WHIST

The almond and the pea fell in love and had a baby.
They named her Peanut.

My grandpa named his dogs Timex, Rolex, and
Swatch.
Those are his watch dogs.

From a real court transcript:
Question: So, besides your wife and children, do you
have any other animals or pets?

My dog is a magician. He's a labracadabrador.

SIGN ON RESTAURANT DOOR:

"We love kids, but please keep them at your table.
Unattended kids will be given a shot of espresso and
a free puppy."

FAMILY PET NAMES

```
G Q Z L X J X G F K U C C O O P E R C V
R O V A U U E A Y Z H Y S Z F Z I R Y W
U Y M Y I C P L N A B C X Y M D C U Q J
I N P U M P Y Y R X I I S X I Z R L I A
X R S V M H V L H Z I N O V I S I I V O
M C V T E D I J P N M K L B U V H L J M
R Q W S Q E R Q J U F J H X W X V Y K J
E B E N T L E Y T M J O S G E M P D G J
C U N R B L K K K U D A S Q D W F R N L
Q Y H B M H N E W H V G E C O L I V E R
H P E A N U T E B B L W Q A W T F S C
V C P L G D M C U W Q F E B C H C E G P
N M P U X B I D M R F C S Y G T A W F I
Y N N E P E D M C D H E R K E Y X R D W
N W D O S Y U B L V L U Q T P L V A Y D
B U X I E G V T T H K S V L W U I Q W C
H O Y R Z U V O U W S C V W H S U A O L
P Y U G Y E P N D S O N Q Q Y R R C B N
O E I D A S C G H C X X I E P Z A N S A
H N P J W X J T I H C Y K C U L C G A U
```

BAILEY	DAISY	OLIVER
BENTLEY	LILY	PEANUT
BUDDY	LUCKY	PENNY
CHARLIE	LUCY	SADIE
COOPER	MAX	SPOT

A bear walks into a restaurant and says, "I'd like a grilled..............cheese."

"What's with the big pause?" the waiter asks.

"I'm a bear."

Q: What hotel did the cheese stay in?
A: The Stilton.

When asked how Swiss cheese is made, the dad said, "From hole milk."

Our family is like a fine cheese.
We get funkier with age.

Did you hear the joke about the pepperoni pizza?
Never mind. It's way too cheesy.

Did you hear about the dad who sliced his fingers while cutting cheese?

It was indicative of grater problems.

WHO CUT THE CHEESE?

```
L B O B V B Y G I Z Q R P O M E R Y O K
J S S R X Q K N O C R E A M N N I V G K
J F N B J B T D F A S U R D S Y U R S A
N T U A O X S F Q D T I M C Z B W T B G
Y N K J X U X X Z O R G I O R M E A G L
E U L B W V T S I T I Q G X N Q S O H J
F U D H L E T L H J N K I P Y V U W P U
B O R M E I Y E U C G I A K M D H F C E
M W Z B L A S R V X C P N F A X R H S H
A F E T Q U V L O A H P O A J E Y Z E Q
R A O I X W L T F Q E O G E H C N A M I
U N B W L G K I C I E S A I X P L M E C
A M J F Y W Y V U T S K N Q O Y O Z F E
J U K F I T H P S W E C A G O N G J A B
R A F X J A L W T A P A Z B U R A S X J
B U C I E L Q Z Q J A O Y H U C I M U Y
C U D K W W H F M O R I D Y O A J U O H
C N Y N V B M S O W U K E S G D X B G R
Z H F W Q U B H O S T R Z O V J I K S U
L B J Q Q O V X T W E N O P R A C S A M
```

ASIAGO

BLUE

BRIE

CREAM

GOAT

GOUDA

GRUYÈRE

JACK

MANCHEGO

MASCARPONE

ORMEA

PARMIGIANO

ROMANO

STILTON

STRING CHEESE

"I used to wonder why I had hair on my legs, but now
I know it's for my toddler sons and daughters
to pull themselves up off the ground
with as I scream in pain."
–Jim Gaffigan

———————————

"When you're young, you think your dad is Superman.
Then you grow up, and you realize he's just a regular
guy who wears a cape."
–Dave Attell

———————————

"I love being married. I was single for a long time, and
I just got so sick of finishing my own sentences."
–Brian Kiley

———————————

"There should be a children's song: 'If You're Happy
and You Know It, Keep It to Yourself
and Let Your Dad Sleep.'"
–Jim Gaffigan

———————————

"Nothing in life is fun for the whole family. There are
no massage parlors with ice cream and free jewelry."
–Jerry Seinfeld

STAND-UP COMEDY

```
P G M P K N L O S I W L V J U Q X J T W
N O I T A S I V O R P M I Q J J B T L D
G N I F F I R O J V L C U E B C O P Z E
D F P N S P V Q W K O L T I W Y Q G E R
S S O O W Y U O Q T Q O U Q U Q L J H K
X O X A N U I N Y G N N I M T I M I N G
G D W T C S P N C O N N E C T O R L A J
C X Z L E I B D N H O N Z J B B Z N V C
W G A G S G E O E N L N V M N V Z A N G
X F U T W T Y X D W C I R P R Z D O E N
K E E Q C I Q Z V O Q X N L P Y I N V A
U A L A N E W J Y F Z C U E B S D E D I
A T N R T G V B A G Y X I R S P Y L C D
P E X A O U V V F W U Y P E Z A S I U E
R Z F D M A R K K G Y M R B Y P E N K M
W O H S Q Z S E A G X P J I P E Q E W O
C U Y R N N F T R C M A M L H C B R C C
T C A S S U M P T I O N D Y G H E J G H
M A G I R Y S W S U J O Z J U R A A R U
D T W F K J Z P I A O X V C O J T I J H
```

ASSUMPTION   FEATURE   RIFFING
BEAT   IMPRESSION   ROAST
COMEDIAN   IMPROVISATION   SEGUE
CONNECTOR   ONE-LINER   SHOW
ENACTED   PUNCH LINE   TIMING

One day while he was building a barn, a cowboy lost his favorite book. A week later, one of his horses came up to him holding the book in its mouth. The cowboy was stunned. He took the book from the horse and said, "It's a miracle!"

"Not exactly," said the horse. "Your name is written inside."

A three-legged dog walks into a saloon in the Old West. He slides up to the bar and announces, "I'm looking for the man who shot my paw."

Knock-knock!
Who's there?
Amarillo.
Amarillo who?
Amarillo-fashioned cowboy!

Q: Why do cowboys put big hats and boots on their salads?
A: They prefer ranch dressing.

CLINT EASTWOOD MOVIES

```
E L E M A N R E V I R C I T S Y M C F X
N U X V V E V Z O G G I V L Y V I X F T
L X S Y R I M B B Y R R A H Y T R I D I
J E X B T U M Z X J Z C U R Y U E J J E
H Z B X N G C X H Z E L H H E U P M T T
H R V W P M I E I E D S E E J J O G C X
G H B M R G P G L X R A P V C J R Q J G
J I V H A Z H G G B T E P W D R T I V V
X T N I M H T Z T P U T A D B H H I K F
F E M I R C E U R T F O K F T W G N N W
J D Z Q U W Y U I H A I R T T L I V S E
B Q N P B Y A S G E F T M T K E T I O R
P S J M E R E D I R E L A P J C R C W X
S M J O P I N K C A D I L L A C V T R X
D V G O R U O C E A C Y L A F C S U Y I
R B B O Z O F E P U S D R V W K B S Q Q
P V K B R S J A Q U P R V D J E D G A R
G Q D E N A X N L O N I R O T N A R G B
F D H H S J S L X P S I X J D Y P D N G
N T B I I V Y N X F B F B G G C M T T F
```

BIRD	INVICTUS	SULLY
CITY HEAT	J. EDGAR	THE ROOKIE
DIRTY HARRY	MYSTIC RIVER	TIGHTROPE
GRAN TORINO	PALE RIDER	TROUBLE CURVE
HEREAFTER	PINK CADILLAC	TRUE CRIME

A guy goes into a butcher shop and bets the butcher $50 that he couldn't reach the meat on the top shelf. "No way," said the butcher. "The steaks are too high."

Waiter: Do you want a box for your burger?
Dad: No, but I'll wrestle you for the fries!

Did you hear about the restaurant on the moon? The food is great but there's no atmosphere.

I went to a restaurant, and it had Salisbury steak on the menu. I excitedly called over the waiter and asked him to wipe it off.

Waitress: Soup or salad?
Dad: Super salad? I'll just have a regular one.

Girlfriend: This restaurant's waiters are as terrible as its website.
Boyfriend: I guess it just has a problem with servers.

STEAKHOUSE

```
G L K R B H Y K Y R F Z X P B P U R T H
E Y O L M I A F Q Y G I E H Z W Z P E M
L Z C N A N Q J W H O N M L W V U V L Z
D P E E G X F S P K Y M K C A B T U O I
D L D U U H S H C J O M S S B S E G J N
I A S I N G O A R D E I C J P M G T C L
R C M C F B V R Y Z U I X S X Y M C B F
G E O I Q Z F X N T M B H L A E V S V C
U O V Z O C M Y U O M L E F D F O J F H
K U E H U Q M T O I T F R M D J R A K O
G C W D P K S R G P A O N Z P H N W Z P
V C E U Y R G A N C H G E F O N I D V H
B E X H Y N L L X L A O H Y T X L M K O
M O P X I L B T M E B D O S A N A S B U
G O P N G A P E I P T E B K T F J K C S
I B I F S N C I C P V C N O O S J Z H E
V D B I S T R O G B V H R R E N I D I F
S D B A R B E C U E M A K X S W V Q Q S
T Y K U U N R L X V A O R H T A I U W X
D L E T N A P W K O I I J X P Z O N G X
```

ANGUS	COOK	LONGHORN
BARBECUE	DINER	OUTBACK
BISTRO	DINING ROOM	PLACE
CAFÉ	FOGO DE CHAO	POTATOES
CHOPHOUSE	GRIDDLE	TEXAS

If Iron Man and the Silver Surfer teamed up, would they be allies. . . or alloys?

Q: What does Clark Kent use to keep the sun out of his eyes?
A: A supervisor.

Batman walks into a bar.
"What'll you have?" the bartender asks.
Batman growls, "Just ice."

Q: What does Thor wear under his costume?
A: Thunderpants.

Boss: We need to talk about your workplace attire.
Employee: Why? Haven't you heard the phrase "dress for the job you want"?
Boss: Yes, but that doesn't mean you can come to work in a Spider-Man costume.

COMIC BOOK HEROES

```
A U G K P A V F Q F J A G O T H H T X L
W M W C D M W P D D E R D E G D U J Z J
K K G U C A P T A M E R I C A H U L K Q
D W R L L X Y N P Q G C M W W U W V Y G
L B Z Y R G O L A B D D M F H N W V P R
S B B D X I B Q V M N R V A K O D H X E
B R G A O I G S X U A N C Z R W S X B E
S J E L E Y S T R W W U C E P V F T E N
Q Y B G T P B E A Z Y K Q F A L E W I L
D H Y A N I F S O B H L M A X V X L I A
V R P R X A E W W M Z Q P S C Y P E N N
T O O H X I R X Q N O A G J J H P S W T
T J C R A V Y R N A M N O R I Y T W I E
V U O X V W B C E G D X L O J X R X R R
W H B J W G K H B W T G Q U Q Z S L D N
T A O R O V V E E C O C M A D F U O C Q
C M R X Z K N F Y M R P Y J X C B J Y L
M E S N X Q E T I E Q V Y V A N T M A N
R P G H L J U R P Y F Z T Y C H O U A C
F N E B R D X V K F C N Q M K N O U N S
```

ANT-MAN
AQUAMAN
BATGIRL
CAPT. AMERICA
GREEN LANTERN

HAWKEYE
HULK
IRON MAN
JOKER
JUDGE DREDD

LADY LUCK
MARVEL
POWER RANGERS
ROBOCOP
THOR

Q: Why do dramatic teenagers hang out in groups of 3, 5, or 7?
A: Because they can't even.

Dad: What're you up to?
Son: Just thinking.
Dad: Ah, that must be what I smelled burning.

HOW TO EMBARRASS YOUR KIDS

```
F Q V E S Y S N Q B Y X C O X I C X A V
I A D F S S Z A J E R L E S A E T V L T
I A S N I H L D S I E Q T L O I N Y A G
L H O N K I M A I N K O K J F Y D X U Y
D L S M X X V X N G C T K E G I Q R F M
P X S F U N Q T F G O I Y A R L L S A V
M V X S P H C O V O M J G F C H O J S G
X T I C G V J M L O E Q R E H T V E K F
V S L Y I W M Z V F M O R P O U C U M F
S G Z A C T D U D Y A G F H A Z I O U J
U S O C I A L M E D I A P C K B C C O T
C O C N P E Q A V Y P Y T P W T N B J L
W Z O Q I U N P O Q B W R R D Y G V A O
J W Y S B C B E C A T S J X K O S B U F
H X N S I H K L B I Y E H N E S P T G K
P I H W K P G N I S F I E E E L R N J K
Y J M W G E C V A C E F S H J M V E L F
A E S I T S A H C M P L T X M I V Y V Z
Q B L S X P I K K N E E O Q E S B E J B
S A D P C H E F Q Z Z S C E Q T S Q Z O
```

ACT COOL	MOCKERY	SELFIES
BABY PHOTOS	NICKNAMES	SING
BEING GOOFY	PDAS	SLANG
CHASTISE	PROM	SOCIAL MEDIA
KISS	PUBLIC	TEASE

A father was trying to teach his young son the evils of alcohol. He put one worm in a glass of water and another worm in a glass of whiskey. The worm in the water lived, while the one in the whiskey curled up and died.

"All right, Son," asked the father, "what does that show you?"

"It shows that if you drink alcohol, you will not have worms."

LIES DADS TELL

"I don't have a favorite child."

"I definitely can tell that this is a drawing of a cow."

"I certainly ate my vegetables when I was your age!"

Since I became a dad, I get into trouble more often than when I was a kid. It's mostly when my kids get scolded by their mother for doing something wrong, and they protest, "But Dad does it all the time!"

"Laziness is nothing more than the habit of resting before you get tired."
–Jules Renard

BAD HABITS

```
C L I L S H Z K S P E N D I N G M Q F Z
Y U D A Y D R E A M I N G K B R Z H C Y
D X E V I J J P E P O L G G L C N O G L
L U C S E I A I N P R K I N F I M P E M
O S R G T A J Q G J Y C I A I P Z E A B
T D M M N F E F I Q G R T N L T S S A C
X L D U P C L D P X K S K A G S A C J Z
D U P P X E O E P Y T Q I U E B R E K U
G U R I U Q N L U E Z N C M C I J R H P
I U E P W B J C E O I B A U U G L F V C
I V T R I G W W R N K G I S N L I H L F
T K T T X N S C G T O P N I C Q U I L M
N F I U S I Y H J E U O H I G D H J R H
S N W I J L D O D F D C C D D W S O D A
G O T X K B D I P D U J C I R R K Q T V
X I P C V M V I X O L E S B N U A R J C
X N C N O A D S L S P Y Y K J F K O G Y
T S Z F D R U S S P Y D I G N I N I H W
B D L W H N Y I E M I B C N A K M Q S O
R O I Q B Q I N Z M F S Y V G H K G X U
```

CHEATING	PEN BITING	SPENDING
COMPLAINING	RAMBLING	SWEETS
DAYDREAMING	SLOUCHING	TWITTER
HOARDING	SMOKING	VIDEO GAMES
LYING	SODA	WHINING

Q: What do you call your dad when he falls through the ice?
A: A Pop-sicle.

Daughter: Good night, Daddy!
Dad: It is now!

Q: What's a good snack for dads?
A: Pop-corn.

"Kids! Stop saying I have a dad bod! I'd rather you call it a father figure."

WAYS TO SAY "DAD"

```
V Z M F S C H R S K T X J P S X B L W X
D A D I N A T O R Y A J P P I X M I B O
I T N N P Q C X K Z L I T V W D X M L A
O D Q M W B H A R A N W V E H G D D F H
C K F U C G I L D R P S T R E E M A W Z
H E T A T T E Y R X J M V D V A N G A B
K U P W G H F W W W P J G F N I E N C E
X W L P C V W E K N Z A X D U Q C F L G
G V C T R T D O F L E T P O Q E G J N E
M R E R A E B E R O F C E A S T G E E T
E I X X R M K L G L V O U T B P O N E T
O I I Y O N U D Q D R M O Z F E K Z U E
L N N Z I R W I E D C R C C T S A C Z R
X T A A I J E K H O M L E U B U M R P V
X J M B F F Y T G F I C C S C W A R I E
N M R B E K P F O B W D G Z S P F E W Y
P W E Y F Z V O S F M H D B T H J Z M G
O J P N Y G T Q T M Q P N A H O N Z Q Z
P U U W F K A P U P Q D A C D A P S R H
S W S Q D O B G A L G W Q W V W E R E A
```

ANCESTOR	FOREBEARER	POPS
BEGETTER	FOTER	PUPA
CHIEF	OLD MAN	SUPERMAN
DADDIO	PAPA BEAR	TATEH
DADINATOR	PAW	VIEJO

I was wondering why the ball was getting bigger. Then it hit me.

Four baseball fans—a Cubs fan, a Cardinals fan, a Red Sox fan, and a Yankees fan—are climbing a mountain and arguing about who loves his team more.

The Cubs fan insists he is the most loyal. "This is for the Cubs!" he yells, and jumps off the side of the mountain.

Not to be outdone, the Cardinals fan shouts, "This is for the Cardinals!" and throws himself off the mountain.

The Red Sox fan is next to profess his love for his team. He yells, "This is for everyone!" and pushes the Yankees fan off the mountain.

 @neiltyson

Does it disturb anyone else that "The Los Angeles Angels" baseball team translates directly to "The The Angels Angels"?

MLB TEAMS

```
D B K F A B M W I P W J L E N Q B E T B
R D F J E E S Y I K I X O S D E R Y R Z
L D V P T N G H R S C I T E L H T A O H
T C C S I A S H N F S A G U M Q Y N C N
A Q S L Y K R H M B V C Y G Y S H K K A
K Z R Y Q F Q Y S L A N I D R A C E I M
S A L Q A B T S U Q L N E L O W F E E W
M N S E Z J L T F T Q R A X T Z T S S Q
M O G Q W A E O G V L S J T V R U R D S
D U Y I Y Y V U A T T N J A I W Q G U A
M W E O U Z A Z L R B N U C E O G M E K
U W R Q W K H I O B I D R N O L N M B L
I Y A R Y T A S R K C A S N Q U K A J E
O I G Z K O J A H Z N D Y K P A A U L N
E I Q L H L V T J G Y G B D I C O R V S
H T H P M E A T E H B S L F R K Z D S Z
K Z F B S O V R Y F Z N K I A G O L Z K
L S Z W I F S Q F Z Z Q J O T B S X P M
R F G X W Q J O Z A N P K L E B Z U A H
O K B L O F Y D Z I R H M T S C O P A I
```

ASTROS   MARLINS   RAYS

ATHLETICS   METS   RED SOX

BLUE JAYS   NATIONALS   ROCKIES

BRAVES   PIRATES   ROYALS

CARDINALS   RANGERS   YANKEES

Q: Why was Samuel Morse a terrible poker player?
A: He always telegraphed his hand.

Q: Why do you have to be careful at poker rooms in the jungle?
A: There are so many cheetahs.

Squatting down to get a beer off the bottom shelf of the fridge definitely counts as exercise.

As the president of the Christopher Walken fan club, I can say with certainty that he owns the greatest poker face of all time. It helped him win the 2005 World Series of Poker even though he held only a joker, a 2 of clubs, a 7 of spades, a green number 4 from Uno, and a Monopoly "get out of jail free" card.

You can never win a game against a porcupine. It'll always have the most points.

POKER NIGHT

```
A K U R E X Y D W P Y E N K X J C Y L B
W D E G P P M B U S M S X R C H X E F L
R I V B G C U S Q C J U C R P E W O U J
G G N X I N S G B T H H Z Z G Q D Z H K
U L T G C S I B E W C I Z Q G Z N C C U
R G A B S V C F D P U D P F Z K F T X X
D R W Q G T T T F R O I T S F I G B U G
S R K H N G L H Y U M B C B P H D B P D
M H T M V V O E V N L K U T T Z T S E K
O W T J A I N P C P A B X H P P K K R B
R J G W S O E T T E U Q I T E N R G U Z
Q B W E M V D Q M E X P V Z I D Q N S N
L V J Z D V V U S J N V Y R D X T I A N
T J U Q A Z B P P S Z D D M G Y C N E B
E A I U T X I Q F E T U I M D X G E L L
I U J L X D T R Q Q U O D E M A R V P E
P C V E Z P Y U P Y Y R D P L A Y E R S
N M E J W L O L C X Y H I V T W E F E U
P H W H M B I E M H E J S Y O P Y G C B
G T L W F W B S P T L K F L B O E J B A
```

BEER	DIPS	MUSIC
BLUFFING	DRINKS	PLAYERS
CHIPS	ETIQUETTE	PLEASURE
CIGARS	EVENING	RULES
DECK	MONEY	WINGS

Q: Where's the best place to go Father's Day shopping?
A: Tie-land.

Did you hear about the little boy who was named after his father? They called him Dad.

On Father's Day, a little boy decides to make his dad breakfast in bed. He makes scrambled eggs, toast, and coffee. He brings it to his dad, hands him a cup of coffee, and says, "Try it, Dad!" The father takes a sip and nearly gags because it is so strong. The little boy asks, "Dad, how do you like it?"

Trying not to hurt his feelings, the dad replies, "This is…something else, I've never tasted coffee quite like this before, Son."

The little boy smiles from ear to ear and says, "Drink some more!"

As the father is drinking, he notices two army men in the bottom of the cup. "Hey! Why did you put army men in here?"

The little boy again smiles and sings, "The Best Part of Waking Up Is Soldiers in Your Cup!"

FATHER'S DAY

```
Y B M X P H T P Y X U A Y J Z I Q P E I
W O H F X D G D A G A W D Z S L X B F T
R O V D Q B S I E C Y L B W G E V A G P
K Z Q N A F Y F M S L C E S Q B A L M J
T F W U D Q N J I M W L X R I Z D D L F
C I T T R I H S F I X C A A T F W I E V
D X E V R H S V J R Y K J B X X M N K D
Z X T O S E L Z S P O R T S E P W G W S
O J T M E I S E D D G F P S D S W N A C
R X J E H G R S Z A U D Y Z W L A K M M
Q A F F I Z A Q E V A C A T I O N B Y C
R G P L J C W S C D E L P S C R S Y D F
K K O O V E B Q S F I N L L O D T Q Y W
I J P P N O D N Z A U Q U U V I H M F H
K M W X N D O W T M M C A J F N N I B M
D H I R H R M M N I D T I W M N B Y B C
K E A W D E S S E L B T O A Q E H A A X
T O D C T N O G N Y O T N O C R Q R J D
B R F L O G I D V Z Y V H P F R D Z R C
W M V Z W H X B B D C J J L P S V I M A
```

BALDING   DINNER   RELAX
BASEBALL CAP   FAMILY   SHIRT
BLESSED   FOOT MASSAGE   SPORTS
CARDS   GOLF   TIE
DESSERT   JUNE   VACATION

Jay: You're looking glum.

Tom: Yeah, my doctor says I can't play football anymore.

Jay: Really? I didn't know he'd ever seen you play!

Q: What did the coach say to the broken vending machine?

A: "Give me my quarterback!"

Did you hear about the football team that doesn't have a website?

They can't string three Ws together.

Q: What happens when football players lose their eyesight?

A: They become referees.

@treebro

Why can't I find out anything about this Superb Owl?

FOOTBALL SUNDAY

```
K V B K L J P F A V Z R I B B C O N T Y
A Z U B Y P N D K M S O V T Z H J C Q W
Q O S P T E R S S T E B O C D P G E T D
D N A N Y J H E O P I Z Z A C P K B O B
T T N U O N H M D R F V U R C M F D J Y
A Y C E S I N G L I U Z K Y M N T R E Y
C U T S S O T N I O C R J P V H D B R P
K K U O I R Q A S U U T A T U B D W S Y
L U A F G F S O R Q Z D I M L Q E G E I
E G R U D N Y G L B D F H O C N C E Y F
R B Y U A S R E B O E D F R N R A J R N
V O V S S M U N H K V L G Y R E R D I C
W H W L B U H D E P A K E K J C I B A Q
C Y L M N X M T Z G T G K C B O M D C Q
T E W G S E M I T F L A H Y O R J O S C
O U X F M K X Q M J E L U L R D S V W L
Y G R U G U C Q A G O D D R V B L J E Q
Z A X N W S G A L W V U D I Z R Z G V N
Y E T W P A V W N Y L O L U A G Z U X H
X L Y I P U O D G S O G E N B F B N Z N
```

BEER	HALFTIME	PREDICTION
BETS	HUDDLE	RECORD
CELEBRATION	JERSEY	SANCTUARY
COIN TOSS	LEAGUE	SNACKS
FLAG	PIZZA	TACKLE

A family was at an amusement park. When the young daughter got tired, her dad put her up on his shoulders. But then she started picking at his hair. Wincing, her dad said, "If you keep pulling my hair, you're going to have to get down off my shoulders."

"But Dad," the kid replied, "I'm just trying to get my gum back."

I recently went on an easy ski trip. I got off the chairlift, and it was all downhill from there.

 @LetMeStart

I'm back from a weekend away with the kids. Notice I did not use the word "vacation"? That was deliberate.

Her: This hotel room is too cold.
Him: Go in the corner. It's 90 degrees!

Tourist #1: Why do they call it the Eiffel Tower?
Tourist #2: Because it's an eyeful.

FAMILY VACATION

```
O D A G W K Y K P X T H L R I O K R Z W
N T I N I S W O L W Q A A H J G Y E K H
Z M A P T K I Q D W L T K O K Y S S N V
F O F E I Z O O Y S T T E W P C J O L J
S I Q R R H P N F N J B T G U D H R U D
G K E P A T N J E F G I A A E N H T L B
A W I W T C E M R S N D H W R O W K G K
R T J I U B I R V R R V O N T T L S A V
T N S S N R J K I E S Z E E O G I P P F
Z I D K H G R X U C O A S T V N M R W I
V F U R B X R N L Q D J A B A I P C P S
J M J L A V I U J B P N C R L H C M M H
H V D B T O W X M C A S G L L S U E S I
I U R G N C D N E I Q L T F A A F E L N
R P J P O X X F I A D S L Q R W T O M G
J C T Z W Z S A S P O Y U G T S E Z E H
K G C E J P W I C B E A C H A D H I Q O
D V B I F A S R T X N F R U X M V C S Z
C K L X H Y Z Z L L R Z N P X W E T T H
V N A T I O N A L P A R K L F Z L L L S
```

BALLGAME   HAWAII   RETREAT
BEACH   LAKE TAHOE   REUNION
COAST   NATIONAL PARK   SKIING
FAIR   PUERTO VALLARTA   VISIT
FISHING   RESORT   WASHINGTON D.C.

Daughter: Where are the Himalayas?
Father: If you'd clean your room, you'd know where to find things!

People always say that hard work never killed anybody. Oh yeah? When's the last time you've ever heard of anyone who rested to death?

Knock-knock!
Who's there?
Dew.
Dew who?
Dew something about your room, it's a mess.

Did you hear about the new broom model they just put out?

It's sweeping the nation.

Q: How many kids does it take to change the toilet paper roll?
A: Who knows? No kid has ever done it.

CHORES TO ASSIGN YOUR KIDS

```
U T F E X W P S J T Z P V U M R S Z A L
D R R E K L O T L Y S F D J B Y N J I K
Q I A A L D P H I Z Q W N G S P Y K T Q
G J Z X K B J L T S F O L D I N G U I F
P N A T F I A D T O Q X Q W S Q U T D Z
A T I K O B N T E H D V H R E I B R Y Y
R Z Y P G S Z G R S Q E Q M I C L P B P
Q W E S P J S A B A P O P W H H F E E R
P P K E E O T E O R E L S A E W Q L D R
L W O I L N M L X T F L X Y F B P O R I
V Q I R A M I B O I C W C Z R W O E O Z
I C Q E S I Y A T R J F V T T F T N O S
U V P V D H T T Z H F Q G F E U I Z M V
E Q S I R C M T I J V H C E F L B V B M
D X E L A F T E F A I R D G T R B S V L
N M X E Y V D S C Q C P K J P M K X M R
E J P D J U K U X T E K R E N Q A R D M
O A P K L L U A S T K C E Z G G N I Z Y
X S G X K M G E S T H I M Q R O C W L S
P E E W S E Z N R F V S O M A V B C T L
```

CLEAR TABLE

DELIVERIES

DUST

FEED PETS

FOLDING

GET MAIL

LITTER BOX

MOPPING

RAKING

SET TABLE

SWEEP

TIDY BEDROOM

TRASH

VACUUM

YARD SALE

Tom Cruise made a movie about cooking.
  It's called A Few Good Menus.

My kids wonder why I watch the same Bruce Willis movie every day. But hey, old habits Die Hard.

The best part of the movie is whatever part you missed when you had to take your kid to the bathroom.

Wife: What's this movie about?
Husband: Oh, two hours or so.

Q: How does Darth Vader like his toast?
A: On the dark side.

I applied to Hogwarts School of Witchcraft and Wizardry but never got a response, as it apparently doesn't exist.
Guess I'm going to have to go fight in the Star Wars instead.

ACTION MOVIES

```
O A S G N O K G N I K Z C E R G H T L S
I R V L L J X G H O S T B U S T E R S Y
R K K F H T T M N R Z I I N X J U O L N
A S Z Q H G R M M A N C Q Y U F J F D A
C B I V G G U O A U M U W R U V Y M S O
I J G I G R E K D X N R A Z R J H Q N L
S N X X Q F G A M Z V S E L E T K C E E
B E O T R C R N C B S N W D V H K J I N
Q R Z B I B I E A I I F N A I O H R L T
S S K V N J T Y C M M C J O J P E X A E
M N L B N F A P R S I H G H N H S E A E
S C X A U V A D S E B N R X T X H V C Q
V I M I U R K W Y Z P C I N D J U J I Z
Q U O Y K K V Z A X H O A M V F A S Z O
J F A T S D N G P D Z P O T E X T H K G
C M G S J J A K L U K M K L G G T L C D
N G U D F P G L K C U X P E P D G R X K
X E Q Q R Y O T A G F L V D T I R D C B
T T P R R Q L L Z Z E R X G B V E N O M
Q Z K A J T B I K Y V R X A D B U C V E
```

ALIENS   JAWS   LOOPER
BLACK PANTHER   JUMANJI   SICARIO
GEMINI MAN   JURASSIC PARK   SPIDER-MAN
GHOSTBUSTERS   KING KONG   TRUE GRIT
HEAT   LOGAN   VENOM

People who celebrate Christmas experience four stages of life:

Stage 1: You believe in Santa Claus.
Stage 2: You stop believing in Santa Claus.
Stage 3: You are Santa Claus.
Stage 4: You look like Santa Claus.

 @Dadpression

Pool noodles are a great way to sword fight your kid while still lying on the couch.

We got our daughter a minifridge for her room. I can't wait to see her face light up when she opens it!

 @DadandBuried

Am I proud of myself for letting my kids wake up, play video games, and watch YouTube for 5 hours every summer morning? No.
But am I going to get out of bed and organize activities so they can have fun experiences and we can spend quality time together as a family?
Also no.

WHAT WE LOVE ABOUT DAD

```
P U G M J B A L M P A S S I O N A T E L
L I H A R D W O R K I N G X J E K I V C
O W I L W E S W E C L H I B M W L N M R
I G S T G X S E K V C I T S I M I T P O
H J V U E S X P Q A I Q R T Y V F E F C
C H T N L I U J E I Y T E B D S O G F E
P U D U C X P N R C K O R L P R U R P G
Y Z L R E U E Z G V T O N O E B R I J I
Y C B L M R W Q A U A N P V P C T T F K
F U W P G K P Q H F Z W E S F P B Y C U
D D D E P J B D B U C L L E J L U A R X
I E T E W K Q T I O C O W J T J B S G G
K I F I T Q T J F U Y H L V Y D B G P G
C T J G F N Q I K A W G U G I I S R L Y
L A X V N E E J L A G T Z A G E K O A K
Z I D Y C F F L H O B B L E K K V L Y B
Y Q P W R E N Z A D F Y W O B I Y Z F X
I Y Q E V I T C E T O R P J C N S V U U
B I G H U G S B T X I E Q O R D Y P L G
A S U W A H D A L M H D U Q P U Z D I I
```

BIG HUGS	KIND	PLAYFUL
CLEVER	LAID-BACK	PROTECTIVE
ENERGETIC	LOYAL	RESPECT
HARDWORKING	OPTIMISTIC	SUPPORTIVE
INTEGRITY	PASSIONATE	TALENTED

Q: How did the farmer mend the holes in his jeans?
A: With cabbage patches.

Q: How do you get a lady from a farm to like you?
A: Just a tractor.

A visitor to a farm asked the farmer, "Why does that one pig have a wooden leg?"

"That pig is the bravest pig I ever saw," the farmer replied.

"So why does he have a wooden leg?" the tourist asked.

"One night, our house caught on fire, and he came inside and woke us all up."

"So . . . why does that pig have a wooden leg?"

"You can't eat a pig that brave all at once!"

I support both math and farming.
I guess you could say I'm pro-tractor.

Q: What did the mama cow say to the baby cow?
A: "It's pasture bedtime."

FARM LIFE

```
N Z I L P F L Q L Z Q Y G H L C Y J Y A
A G S X A A D D A C H P B E Y U A O F X
J L N G G R N A X W J O F P Z X S R T H
F E C L V L U T O O I L I A C R E A G E
V T N X I W G R C R G R E G C E F T E E
R A T S G T W Y A G Z W L R I S X D N V
F V O S U W L T S V H V D I V D M Q L W
E I M A W X L I V E S T O C K U E X A F
R T A C R T N X G S L D N U E N L Q N A
U L Z U F J I U F X Q Q Y L W Y M O D D
T U R T K F A M N W D R Z T S R S S Y K
S C D H P Q X F M R T A E U K K M V V C
A N P E B C I K H N G N M R D U I Q N O
P C H K M C O J U W X C S E X S L G S H
E P T Q D E Z O O F Z H A H M A L P P J
M A Q Q N S C S V J Y Q T D I E F N M D
C Q A Y K X V T C A T T L E R E M R A F
A J N U A O N W R K T A S E M W H P I T
L O W I K I H S E C H J G S Q L B T U S
F H X S C O Y O T O P C U M P Z Y B E W
```

ACREAGE	CULTIVATE	LIVESTOCK
AGRICULTURE	FARMER	MILL
CALF	FIELD	PASTURE
CATTLE	GROW	RANCH
COUNTRY	LAND	RURAL

I'm a huge gaming nerd, and people have been telling me to get a life. But that's dumb. I have lots of lives.

Wife: Honey, you should write a book about your life.
Husband: Now that's a novel idea!

I've never gone to a gun range before.
Today, I decided to give it a shot!

Kid: How did you learn to play golf?
Grandpa: I took a golf course.

I bought a coffee table book about the history of forests.
I just like to leaf through the pages.

WHY I LIKE BOWLING SO MUCH:

1. I drink beer.
2. I get a few seconds of exercise.
3. I repeat #1 and #2 for the next couple of hours.

DAD HOBBIES

```
H B G F J L C I A U F S J P Y B U Q U N
N R E P A I R S J O S S Z N K K S X V K
V C Z N F A F Z E G X N B G Q W L M S I
Q D N X X D L A G H M I X Y G V A P W I
C T Z E N N O G C N S N S N V P A S T W
V E D L V H G V W L I X I J H D E R Z B
B Z V K E G S G I M G T J M C Z L R U K
G Y F C T X Q N T M F U N G A H X U L H
I C L U K B J H O I V E I U N L M G S I
B U X L Q E J D L L U I N T H I J X R G
W Z L I O J A T C W A G N V A R T V N D
B P O B T N H S B Y L P T Y P R H I T D
E J M J C G F L B M C U T P L S U Y R O
F T I I I B O W L I N G A A F C R G C W
A S N E J V L S I N G I N G E E I I E S
G G W B D T H V I V L N K B H S H J X W
G N I M A G P V Q F F V R C J Y U E M Z
D O P O V H I K I N G A R C L U L V H N
D O C J S P A I N T B A L L L J X C F S
Z F I I C X P X C D T U W T K V F D C A
```

ARCHERY	GOLF	REPAIRS
BARBECUING	GUITAR	SINGING
BOWLING	HIKING	VINYL
DANCING	HUNTING	WEIGHTLIFTING
GAMING	PAINTBALL	WRITING

Q: What's a missionary's favorite kind of car?
A: A convertible.

A man walks into his psychiatrist's office. "Doctor, you've got to help me," he pleads. "Every night, I dream I'm a fast car. Last night, I dreamed I was a Trans Am. Another night, I was a Ferrari. Before that, I was a Porsche. What does it mean?

"Relax," says the doctor. "You're just having an auto-body experience."

Q: What's a good name for a guy who can never remember where he parked his car?
A: Carlos.

I rushed my wife to the hospital when she started to go into labor, but we didn't make it. She gave birth right there in the car.
It's a boy! We named him Carson.

"I've never had a car accident," said Tom recklessly.

CLASSIC CARS

```
P R P G N F Z W I R B A Z C E Q G G S M
J F A L D O D A U I E N F A I R L A D Y
Z T G Q E X T H T I E S D E L O R E A N
F H A T K S M I P B U V R B M R L J M R
E E N Q D Q I W C H R B Y J K N I J F P
M R I U V O V A I E P Q E F O F G V J K
E C Z G J W L H Y J K G W N C H I R O N
H J O I N L T O V T W B I B T E X V E H
G F N M I D U Z G C A M A R O L D R U M
E I D D W N D B S K A T Q V B B E D D M
R C A F Z M Y R W C G K W C E D S Y M E
E C K J V L C E L N Y F Q M F O R D G T
L C S F M L O E R E L B C Q N N K F U P
X H A V C A C D E E P A F H E O E I K S
I I U A Y Q L T H O C Y O H T R Q Q R U
X O F Z F J Y A R X G R U S R Y V Q C V
O O C B S Z Z S D N N D Q A S E W Y K K
O I E Q H E C U P E L S R K J V C Z T Y
K T Y U N H W E T E T I L E S U T O L G
W H F S E E Q X Q H C P P R E K V C R Y
```

BENTLEY

BENZ

CADILLAC

CAMARO

CHIRON

DELOREAN

EL CAMINO

FAIRLADY

FERRARI

FORD GT

HUDSON HORNET

LOTUS ELITE

PAGANI ZONDA

PORSCHE

VEYRON

After a fish was arrested for swimming without a license, he eventually posted bail. Relieved, he said, "I'm off the hook!"

Q: What do you call a fish with no i?
A: Fsh.

My family ran a major fishing business.
Anybody in the area who wanted to catch or sell any fish had to get permission from Grandpa. That's why they called him the Cod Father.

Neighbor: Do you like fly fishing?
Dad: It's oh-fish-ally the best sport ever!
Neighbor: What's so great about it?
Dad: I don't know, you just get hooked.

Q: What do you call a pelican that isn't any good at catching fish?
A: A pelican't.

FISHING TRIP

```
P L U J O H C N O P T Z A U T X S O O Z
C H G Q J B L D L D I R N D N S O D H X
J W B U T W S S Q U P C Q M P E E D O T
A D S E S O D U T J E K A T I C V V S R
C P N T U A W K N G J I V J M W B L T P
K G O Z N B S E C S D A I X D N D C A F
E J F S J C O J L E C N E I T A P T H L
T S E S S A L G N U S R C F T A B H L B
E D Q R C V R W L K N E E Z L V N A Z K
P J T M Q Y G V O F C L R E C E I O I O
R E S T O O B T C H X I Y I N H S N F T
Y P F W L P H J E X T R A S O C K S Y Y
G E F C G T N S G D R M J A S Z J D J Q
V H C F S W T J S C F B R I K D E I C T
I H X D V J I N O O G F J V O O S A L Z
M P U S U N M O I J G Y Q D O K F R C Y
N E U J L F Y E N I L G N I H S I F L R
G R Q P L W V N O N I M W J N N G P Y Z
G B M M N Y X A J K M N P T C D P X D F
V C U Y J A Z L H H J Z C Y H H U S S G
```

BAIT	HOOKS	RODS
BOOTS	ICE CHEST	SUNGLASSES
EXTRA SOCKS	JACKET	SUNSCREEN
FISHING LINE	PATIENCE	TOWEL
HATS	PONCHO	VEST

Q: What did the hippie tell his friend who said he couldn't stay on his couch anymore?
A: "Namaste."

My wife said I was immature.
So I told her to get out of my fort.

Q: What do you call a bunch of dads hanging out together?
A: A pa-ty.

Q: Why can't DJs play billiards?
A: They always scratch.

Me and this recliner?
Oh yeah, we go way back.

Q: What do cavemen eat for lunch?
A: Club sandwiches.

MAN CAVE

```
S U W L K P C S M S H P A R G O T U A Q
P M G D I H E N U S U P R O J E C T O R
L S P E A K E R S J O Y F R I D G E Y V
A L U U B O M P J O X Q Q T V M E D E I
Q P H A V E N I L H A Q F Q W K X R D B
P P W I X X R T S H A P B O J O U E Q V
G E F C G Y A R G W Q U B R X J S L O A
T O F B V B E J D C L Y E V Z C K Q E U
X A Y W L T M O Z N A N O T D I O M B I
O W C E R X O F O W I S J C F M N H Z H
B X L A I R J U A L S K C A N S N B N E
T K U R H L X E C Y O P Q U O M N J C U
Q Q B N R B D E T G U V W S O M N S Q I
G A H O D I R Y B C N T G J N G A K R M
P Q O A H X E X N A Q F Q T M G W B S I
Z G U D X P K X Y R D E A C I O Z M P W
S R S V X R O G J C A Q B N N N A B F L
O F E U O I P X O A I N D Y W P N V Z L
T B N Y W A B H L D E L S X I V N L L C
Y Y S R A G I C V E C Y H Y C Z S V U V
```

ARCADE	HAVEN	PROJECTOR
AUTOGRAPHS	HIDEAWAY	QUARTERS
CIGARS	LAIR	RECLINER
CLUBHOUSE	POKER	SNACKS
FRIDGE	POOL TABLE	SPEAKERS

SOLUTIONS

(because instructions are always included,
but are usually read as a last resort)

SOLUTIONS

PAGE 3

PAGE 5

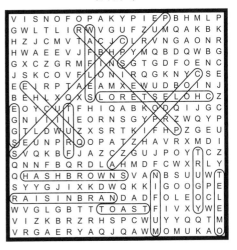

PAGE 7

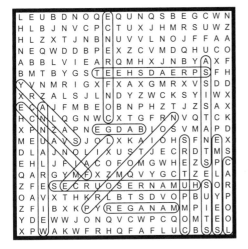

PAGE 9

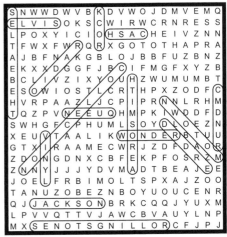

SOLUTIONS

PAGE 11

PAGE 13

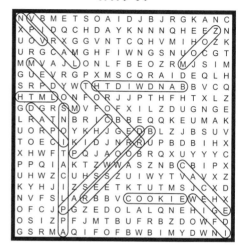

PAGE 15

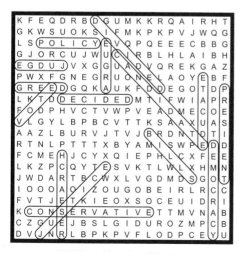

PAGE 17

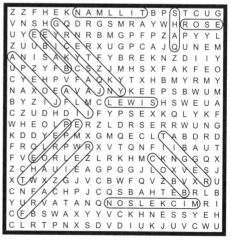

SOLUTIONS

PAGE 19

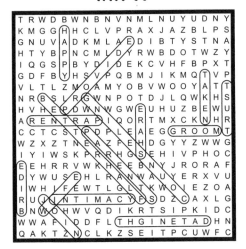

PAGE 21

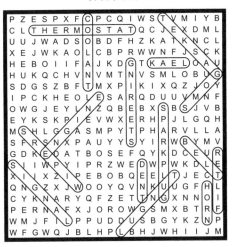

PAGE 23

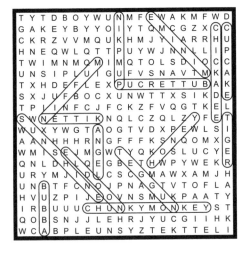

PAGE 25

SOLUTIONS

PAGE 27

PAGE 29

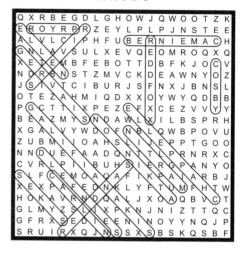

PAGE 31

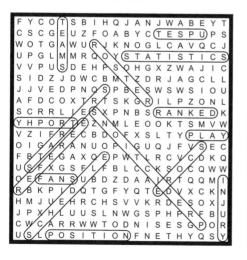

PAGE 33

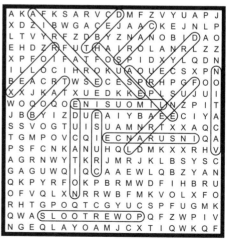

SOLUTIONS

PAGE 35

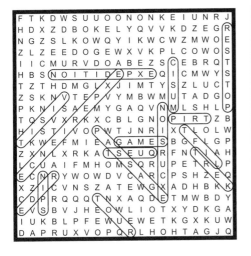

PAGE 37

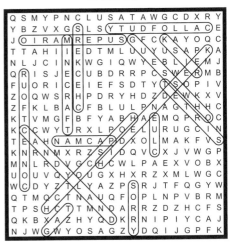

PAGE 39

PAGE 41

SOLUTIONS

PAGE 43

PAGE 45

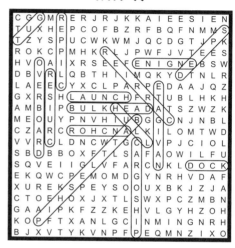

PAGE 47

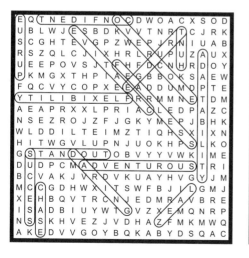

PAGE 49

SOLUTIONS

PAGE 51

PAGE 53

PAGE 55

PAGE 57

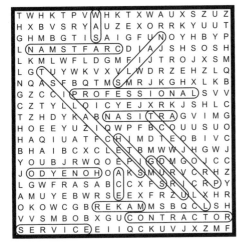

SOLUTIONS

PAGE 59

PAGE 61

PAGE 63

PAGE 65

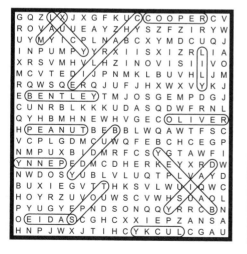

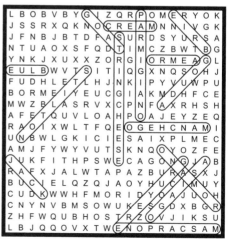

SOLUTIONS

PAGE 67

PAGE 69

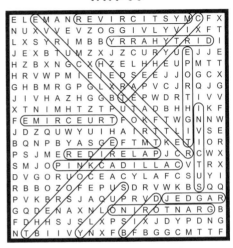

PAGE 71

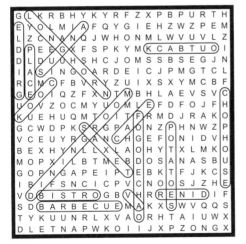

PAGE 73

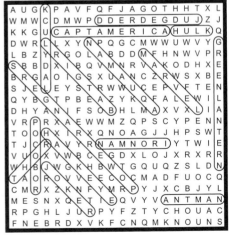

SOLUTIONS

PAGE 75

PAGE 77

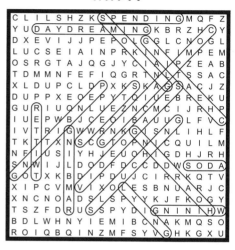

PAGE 79

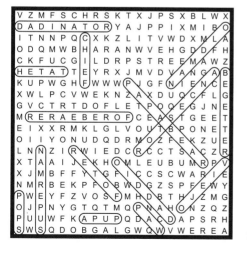

PAGE 81

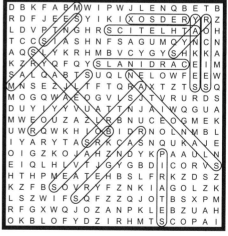

SOLUTIONS

PAGE 83

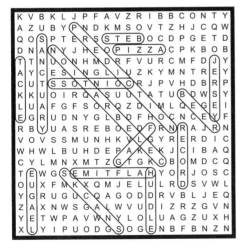

PAGE 85

PAGE 87

PAGE 89

SOLUTIONS

PAGE 91

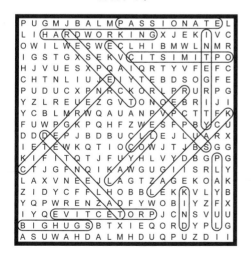

PAGE 93

PAGE 95

PAGE 97

SOLUTIONS

PAGE 99

PAGE 101

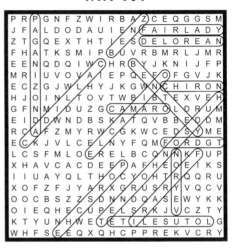

PAGE 103

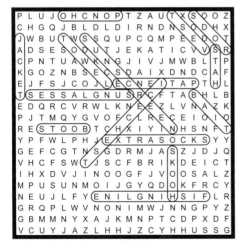

PAGE 105

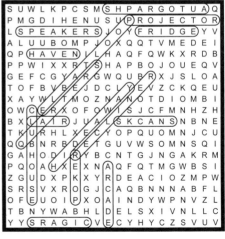